JOURNEYS IN LITERATURE
British and World Classics

D

K12
A Stride Company

BOOK STAFF & CONTRIBUTORS

John Holdren *Senior Vice President for Content and Curriculum*
Beth Zemble *Director, Alternative Learning Strategies; Director, Language Arts*
Cynthia Guidici *Content Specialist*
Marianne Murphy *Content Specialist*
Tim Mansfield *Writer*
Suzanne Montazer *Senior Art Director*
David Reinhold *Print Designer*
Sarah McMullen *Cover Designer*
Stephanie Shaw *Illustrator*
Jean Stringer *Rights Specialist*
Annette Scarpitta *Media Editor*
Joel Storer *Text Editor*
Elia Ben-Ari *Text Editor*
Mary Beck Desmond *Text Editor*
Sarah Allard *Project Manager*

Bror Saxberg *Chief Learning Officer*
John Holdren *Senior Vice President for Content and Curriculum*
Maria Szalay *Senior Vice President for Product Development*
David Pelizzari *Senior Director, Product Development*
Kim Barcas *Creative Director*
Jeff Burridge *Managing Editor*
Sally Russell *Senior Manager, Media*
Chris Frescholtz *Senior Project Manager, High School*
Corey Maender *Director, Program Management*
Lisa Dimaio Iekel *Production Manager*
John G. Agnone *Director of Publications*

Cover: Based on photos of the London skyline. Lance Bellers/Dreamstime; Tower Bridge. ©
Oliver Malms/iStockphoto

At Stride, Inc. (NYSE: LRN)—formerly K12 Inc.—we are reimagining lifelong learning as a rich, deeply
personal experience that prepares learners for tomorrow. Since its inception, Stride has been committed
to removing barriers that impact academic equity and to providing high-quality education for anyone—
particularly those in underserved communities. The company has transformed the teaching and
learning experience for millions of people by providing innovative, high-quality, tech-enabled education
solutions, curriculum, and programs directly to students, schools, the military, and enterprises in primary,
secondary, and post-secondary settings. Stride is a premier provider of K-12 education for students,
schools, and districts, including career learning services through middle and high school curriculum.
Providing a solution to the widening skills gap in the workplace and student loan crisis, Stride equips
students with real world skills for in-demand jobs with career learning. For adult learners, Stride delivers
professional skills training in healthcare and technology, as well as staffing and talent development
for Fortune 500 companies. Stride has delivered millions of courses over the past decade and serves
learners in all 50 states and more than 100 countries. The company is a proud sponsor of the Future
of School, a nonprofit organization dedicated to closing the gap between the pace of technology and
the pace of change in education. More information can be found at stridelearning.com, K12.com,
destinationsacademy.com, galvanize.com, techelevator.com, and medcerts.com.

ISBN 978-1-60153-036-3   Printed in U.S.A.

Printed by Total Printing Systems, Newton, IN, USA, August 2022.

CONTENTS

HEROIC BATTLES

THE CANTERBURY TALES

LOVE SONNETS

Romantic Poetry

The Modern Age

Cultures in Conflict

HEROIC
BATTLES

Beowulf and Grendel

Anonymous, translated by Seamus Heaney

Beowulf is an epic poem, written in Old English, by an author or authors who are now unknown. Scholars date the oldest Beowulf manuscript between the eighth and eleventh centuries, though it is likely that the poem was shared via the oral tradition for centuries before it was written down.

The poem tells the story of Hrothgar, a Danish king, who reigns during a time of prosperity. He builds a feasting hall called Heorot where his warriors can hold celebrations and listen to songs. The noise emanating from Heorot infuriates a monstrous demon named Grendel, who is the antagonist of this poem. Grendel subsequently rampages throughout the kingdom for 12 years, slaughtering Danes and defying all their attempts to subdue his treachery.

News of the Danish predicament reaches Beowulf, a young Geatish warrior, whose father had once received a favor from Hrothgar. Beowulf sails to Denmark, armed with a small group of warriors, prepared to defeat the monstrous Grendel. Hrothgar receives him warmly and holds a great feast at Heorot to honor Beowulf. During that feast, the Geat boasts of his former accomplishments to answer a challenge posed by Unferth, one of the Danes.

The excerpt here begins when Hrothgar departs Heorot and leaves Beowulf awaiting Grendel's attack.

Hrothgar departed then with his house-guard.
The lord of the Shieldings, their shelter in war,
left the mead-hall to lie with Wealhtheow,
his queen and bedmate. The King of Glory   665

Hrothgar: a legendary king of the Danes
house-guard: bodyguards
Shieldings: Danes
mead-hall: feasting hall
Wealhtheow: Hrothgar's wife

(as people learned) had posted a lookout
who was a match for Grendel, a guard against
    monsters,
special protection to the Danish prince.
And the Geat placed complete trust
in his strength of limb and the Lord's favor.   670
He began to remove his iron breast-mail,
took off the helmet and handed his attendant
the patterned sword, a smith's masterpiece,
ordering him to keep the equipment guarded.
And before he bedded down, Beowulf,   675 *Beowulf renounces*
that prince of goodness, proudly asserted: *the use of weapons*
"When it comes to fighting, I count myself
as dangerous any day as Grendel.
So it won't be a cutting edge I'll wield
to mow him down, easily as I might.   680
He has no idea of the arts of war,
of shield or sword-play, although he does possess
a wild strength. No weapons, therefore,
for either this night: unarmed he shall face me
if face me he dares. And may the Divine Lord   685
in His wisdom grant the glory of victory
to whichever side He sees fit."

Then down the brave man lay with his bolster   *The Geats await*
under his head and his whole company   *Grendel's attack*
of sea-rovers at rest beside him.   690
None of them expected he would ever see
his homeland again or get back
to his native place and the people who reared him.
They knew too well the way it was before,

Grendel: the monstrous villain in *Beowulf*
Geat: Beowulf
breast-mail: protective armor worn over one's chest
smith: blacksmith
a cutting edge: a sword
bolster: a pad or cushion
sea-rovers: the men who had sailed with Beowulf

how often the Danes had fallen prey   695
to death in the mead-hall. But the Lord was
        weaving
a victory on His war-loom for the Weather-Geats.
Through the strength of one they all prevailed;
they would crush their enemy and come through
in triumph and gladness. The truth is clear: 700
Almighty God rules over mankind
and always has.
                        Then out of the night
came the shadow-stalker, stealthy and swift;
the hall-guards were slack, asleep at their posts,
all except one; it was widely understood   705
that as long as God disallowed it,
the fiend could not bear them to his
        shadow-bourne.
One man, however, was in fighting mood,
awake and on edge, spoiling for action.

In off the moors, down through the mist bands   710   *Grendel strikes*
God-cursed Grendel came greedily loping.
The bane of the race of men roamed forth,
hunting for a prey in the high hall.
Under the cloud-murk he moved towards it
until it shone above him, a sheer keep   715
of fortified gold. Nor was that the first time
he had scouted the grounds of Hrothgar's
        dwelling—
although never in his life, before or since,
did he find harder fortune or hall-defenders.
Spurned and joyless, he journeyed on ahead   720

---

shadow-bourne: dark or shadowy stream
spoiling: eager
moors: marshes; swampy areas
loping: moving quickly and easily
bane: curse
a sheer keep: a tall fortress
spurned: scorned

and arrived at the bawn. The iron-braced door
turned on its hinge when his hands touched it.
Then his rage boiled over, he ripped open
the mouth of the building, maddening for blood,
pacing the length of the patterned floor   725
with his loathsome tread, while a baleful light,
flame more than light, flared from his eyes.
He saw many men in the mansion, sleeping,
a ranked company of kinsmen and warriors
quartered together. And his glee was demonic,   730
picturing the mayhem: before morning
he would rip life from limb and devour them,
feed on their flesh; but his fate that night
was due to change, his days of ravening
had come to an end.   735

                     Mighty and canny,   *A Geat warrior*
Hygelac's kinsman was keenly watching   *perishes*
for the first move the monster would make.
Nor did the creature keep him waiting
but struck suddenly and started in;
he grabbed and mauled a man on his bench,   740
bit into his bone-lappings, bolted down his blood
and gorged on him in lumps, leaving the body
utterly lifeless, eaten up
hand and foot. Venturing closer,
his talon was raised to attack Beowulf   745
where he lay on the bed; he was bearing in
with open claw when the alert hero's
comeback and armlock forestalled him utterly.
The captain of evil discovered himself   *Beowulf's fight*
in a handgrip harder than anything   750   *with Grendel*

---

bawn: a defensive wall
baleful: menacing or threatening
ravening: preying on others
canny: shrewd or clever
Hygelac: a relative and lord of Beowulf, to whom Beowulf owes
    allegiance
bone-lappings: joints
talon: claw

he had ever encountered in any man
on the face of the earth. Every bone in his body
quailed and recoiled, but he could not escape.
He was desperate to flee to his den and hide
with the devil's litter, for in all his days   755
he had never been clamped or cornered like this.
Then Hygelac's trusty retainer recalled
his bedtime speech, sprang to his feet
and got a firm hold. Fingers were bursting,
the monster back-tracking, the man overpowering.   760
The dread of the land was desperate to escape,
to take a roundabout road and flee
to his lair in the fens. The latching power
in his fingers weakened; it was the worst trip
the terror-monger had taken to Heorot.   765
And now the timbers trembled and sang,
a hall-session that harrowed every Dane
inside the stockade: stumbling in fury,
the two contenders crashed through the building.
The hall clattered and hammered, but somehow   770
survived the onslaught and kept standing:
it was handsomely structured, a sturdy frame
braced with the best of blacksmith's work
inside and out. The story goes
that as the pair struggled, mead-benches were   775
    smashed
and sprung off the floor, gold fittings and all.
Before then, no Shielding elder would believe
there was any power or person upon earth
capable of wrecking their horn-rigged hall
unless the burning embrace of a fire   780

---

quailed: trembled; squirmed
recoiled: pulled away
litter: companions; company; in this case, other monsters like
    Grendel
retainer: servant
fens: marshes
stockade: fort
horn-rigged: horn covered

engulf it in flame. Then an extraordinary
wail arose, and bewildering fear
came over the Danes. Everyone felt it
who heard that cry as it echoed off the wall,
a God-cursed scream and strain of catastrophe,   785
the howl of the loser, the lament of the hell-serf
keening his wound. He was overwhelmed,
manacled tight by the man who of all men
was foremost and strongest in the days of this life.

But the earl-troop's leader was not inclined   790 *Beowulf's thanes*
to allow his caller to depart alive: *defend him*
he did not consider that life of much account
to anyone anywhere. Time and again,
Beowulf's warriors worked to defend
their lord's life, laying about them   795
as best they could with their ancestral blades.
Stalwart in action, they kept striking out
on every side, seeking to cut
straight to the soul. When they joined the struggle
there was something they could not have known   800
    at the time,
that no blade on earth, no blacksmith's art
could ever damage their demon opponent.
He had conjured the harm from the cutting edge
of every weapon. But his going away
out of this world and the days of his life   805
would be agony to him, and his alien spirit
would travel far into fiends' keeping.

Then he who had harrowed the hearts of men   *Grendel is*
with pain and affliction in former times   *defeated,*
                                              Beowulf fulfils his
                                              boast

---

keening: mournfully wailing
manacled: bound; shackled
account: worth
stalwart: bold; vigorous
conjured the harm from: magically removed the danger from
harrowed: agonized

and had given offence also to God   810
found that his bodily powers failed him.
Hygelac's kinsman kept him helplessly
locked in a handgrip. As long as either lived,
he was hateful to the other. The monster's whole
body was in pain, a tremendous wound   815
appeared on his shoulder. Sinews split
and the bone-lappings burst. Beowulf was granted
the glory of winning; Grendel was driven
under the fen-banks, fatally hurt,
to his desolate lair. His days were numbered,   820
the end of his life was coming over him,
he knew it for certain; and one bloody clash
had fulfilled the dearest wishes of the Danes.
The man who had lately landed among them,
proud and sure, had purged the hall,   825
kept it from harm; he was happy with his
     nightwork
and the courage he had shown. The Geat captain
had boldly fulfilled his boast to the Danes:
he had healed and relieved a huge distress,
unremitting humiliations,   830
the hard fate they'd been forced to undergo,
no small affliction. Clear proof of this
could be seen in the hand the hero displayed
high up near the roof: the whole of Grendel's
shoulder and arm, his awesome grasp.   835

Then morning came and many a warrior   *The morning after:*
gathered, as I've heard, around the gift-hall,   *relief and*
clan-chiefs flocking from far and near   *rejoicings*
down wide-ranging roads, wondering greatly
at the monster's footprints. His fatal departure   840
was regretted by no-one who witnessed his trail,

---

sinews: muscles
desolate lair: lonely hideout
purged: cleansed
unremitting: ceaseless

the ignominious marks of his flight
where he'd skulked away, exhausted in spirit
and beaten in battle, bloodying the path,
hauling his doom to the demons' mere. 845
The bloodshot water wallowed and surged,
there were loathsome upthrows and overturnings
of waves and gore and wound-slurry.
With his death upon him, he had dived deep
into his marsh-den, drowned out his life 850
and his heathen soul: hell claimed him there.

Then away they rode, the old retainers
with many a young man following after,
a troop on horseback, in high spirits
on their bay steeds. Beowulf's doings 855
were praised over and over again.
Nowhere, they said, north or south
between the two seas or under the tall sky
on the broad earth was there anyone better
to raise a shield or to rule a kingdom. 860
Yet there was no laying of blame on their lord,
the noble Hrothgar; he was a good king.

---

ignominious: humiliating; disgraceful
skulked: crept
mere: marsh
wallowed: whirled
wound-slurry: a liquid mixture of blood, torn muscle, and water
heathen: godless
bay steeds: horses

9

HEKTOR AND ACHILLEUS

Homer, translated by Richmond Lattimore

The Iliad *is an ancient Greek epic poem that tells the story of the tenth year of the Trojan War. This protracted conflict between Greece and the ancient city-state of Troy was instigated by a great wrong that Paris, a Trojan prince, did to Greece when he carried away Helen, the wife of King Menelaus of the Greek city-state of Sparta.*

The Greeks united under the leadership of Agamemnon, the brother of Menelaus, to attack the Trojans. During the nine years of the conflict, the determined Greek army surrounded the city of Troy. Many fierce battles were fought outside the gates, and the victory shifted from one side to the other. Oftentimes, the Greeks plundered neighboring kingdoms friendly to Troy while part of the army remained to guard the city.

In this excerpt, Hektor, Paris's brother and the greatest warrior of Troy, battles Achilleus, the mightiest Greek warrior. Achilleus is especially angered because Hektor has slain his dearest friend and comrade, Patroklus. The story here begins when the goddess Athene, disguised as another of Hektor's brothers, Deïphobos, cunningly urges Hektor to meet Achilleus outside the protection of the city's walls.

"My brother, it is true our father and the lady our mother, taking
my knees in turn, and my companions about me, entreated
that I stay within, such was the terror upon all of them.
But the heart within me was worn away by hard sorrow for you.
But now let us go straight on and fight hard, let there be no   5
    sparing
of our spears, so that we can find out whether Achilleus
will kill us both and carry our bloody war spoils back
to the hollow ships, or will himself go down under your spear."

---

entreated: pleaded
Achilleus: the Greek hero of the Trojan War; also known as Achilles

So Athene spoke and led him on by beguilement.
Now as the two in their advance were come close together,   10
first of the two to speak was tall helm-glittering Hektor:
"Son of Peleus, I will no longer run from you, as before this
I fled three times around the great city of Priam, and dared not
stand to your onfall. But now my spirit in turn has driven me
to stand and face you. I must take you now, or I must be taken.   15
Come then, shall we swear before the gods? For these are the
      highest
who shall be witnesses and watch over our agreements.
Brutal as you are I will not defile you, if Zeus grants
to me that I can wear you out, and take the life from you.
But after I have stripped your glorious armor, Achilleus,   20
I will give your corpse back to the Achaians. Do you do likewise."
      Then looking darkly at him swift-footed Achilleus answered:
"Hektor, argue me no agreements. I cannot forgive you.
As there are no trustworthy oaths between men and lion,
nor wolves and lambs have spirit that can be brought to   25
      agreement
but forever these hold feelings of hate for each other,
so there can be no love between you and me, nor shall there be
oaths between us, but one or the other must fall before then
to glut with his blood Ares the god who fights under the shield's
      guard.
Remember every valor of yours, for now the need comes   30
hardest upon you to be a spearman and a bold warrior.
There shall be no more escape for you, but Pallas Athene

Athene: in Greek mythology, a goddess who inspires mortals to act heroically; also
      known as Athena and Pallas Athena
beguilement: trickery; deception
Peleus: father of Achilleus
Priam: the king of Troy and Hektor's father
defile: besmirch; taint or tarnish the reputation of another
Zeus: in Greek mythology, the king of the gods
Achaians: the Greeks
glut: overfill
Ares: in Greek mythology, the god of war
valor: courage; bravery

will kill you soon by my spear. You will pay in a lump for all those

sorrows of my companions you killed in your spear's fury."
   So he spoke, and balanced the spear far shadowed, and 35 threw it;

but glorious Hektor kept his eyes on him, and avoided it,

for he dropped, watchful, to his knee, and the bronze spear flew over his shoulder

and stuck in the ground, but Pallas Athene snatched it, and gave it

back to Achilleus, unseen by Hektor shepherd of the people.

But now Hektor spoke out to the blameless son of Peleus: 40

"You missed; and it was not, O Achilleus like the immortals,

from Zeus that you knew my destiny; but you thought so; or rather

you are someone clever in speech and spoke to swindle me,

to make me afraid of you and forget my valor and war strength.

You will not stick your spear in my back as I run away from you 45

but drive it into my chest as I storm straight in against you;

if the god gives you that; and now look out for my brazen

spear. I wish it might be taken full length in your body.

And indeed the war would be a lighter thing for the Trojans

if you were dead, seeing that you are their greatest affliction." 50
   So he spoke, and balanced the spear far shadowed, and threw it,

and struck the middle of Peleïdes' shield, nor missed it,

but the spear was driven far back from the shield, and Hektor was angered

because his swift weapon had been loosed from his hand in a vain cast.

He stood discouraged, and had no other ash spear; but lifting 55

his voice he called aloud on Deïphobos of the pale shield,

and asked him for a long spear, but Deïphobos was not near him.

---

swindle: trick
brazen: made of brass-colored metal
Peleïdes' shield: the shield of Achilleus
cast: throw
Deïphobos: Hektor's brother and fellow prince of Troy

And Hektor knew the truth inside his heart, and spoke aloud:
"No use. Here at last the gods have summoned me deathward.
I thought Deïphobos the hero was here close beside me, 60
but he is behind the wall and it was Athene cheating me,
and now evil death is close to me, and no longer far away,
and there is no way out. So it must long since have been pleasing
to Zeus, and Zeus' son who strikes from afar, this way; though
    before this
they defended me gladly. But now my death is upon me. 65
Let me at least not die without a struggle, inglorious,
but do some big thing first, that men to come shall know of it."
    So he spoke, and pulling out the sharp sword that was slung
at the hollow of his side, huge and heavy, and gathering
himself together, he made his swoop, like a high-flown eagle 70
who launches himself out of the murk of the clouds on the flat
    land
to catch away a tender lamb or a shivering hare; so
Hektor made his swoop, swinging his sharp sword, and
    Achilleus
charged, the heart within him loaded with
    savage fury.
In front of his chest the beautiful elaborate great shield 75
covered him, and with the glittering helm with four horns
he nodded; the lovely golden fringes were shaken about it
which Hephaistos had driven close along the horn of the helmet.
And as a star moves among stars in the night's darkening,
Hesper, who is the fairest star who stands in the sky, such 80
was the shining from the pointed spear Achilleus was shaking
in his right hand with evil intention toward brilliant Hektor.
He was eyeing Hektor's splendid body, to see where it might best
give way, but all the rest of the skin was held in the armor,
brazen and splendid, he stripped when he cut down the 85
    strength of Patroklos;

---

inglorious: shameful
Hephaistos: the Greek god of the forge, where weapons are made
Hesper: the evening star
Patroklos: Achilleus's dear friend and comrade whom Hektor killed

yet showed where the collar-bones hold the neck from the
    shoulders,
the throat, where death of the soul comes most swiftly; in this
    place
brilliant Achilleus drove the spear as he came on in fury,
and clean through the soft part of the neck the spearpoint was
    driven.
Yet the ash spear heavy with bronze did not sever the windpipe, 90
so that Hektor could still make exchange of words spoken.
But he dropped in the dust, and brilliant Achilleus vaunted above
    him:
"Hektor, surely you thought as you killed Patroklos you would be
safe, and since I was far away you thought nothing of me,
O fool, for an avenger was left, far greater than he was,   95
behind him and away by the hollow ships. And it was I;
and I have broken your strength; on you the dogs and the
    vultures
shall feed and foully rip you; the Achaians will bury Patroklos."
    In his weakness Hektor of the shining helm spoke to him:
"I entreat you, by your life, by your knees, by your parents,   100
do not let the dogs feed on me by the ships of the Achaians,
but take yourself the bronze and gold that are there in
    abundance,
those gifts that my father and the lady my mother will give
    you,
and give my body to be taken home again, so that the Trojans
and the wives of the Trojans may give me in death my rite of   105
    burning."
    But looking darkly at him swift-footed Achilleus answered:
"No more entreating of me, you dog, by knees or parents.
I wish only that my spirit and fury would drive me
to hack your meat away and eat it raw for the things that
you have done to me. So there is no one who can hold the   110
    dogs off

---

vaunted: boasted

from your head, not if they bring here and set before me ten
     times
and twenty times the ransom, and promise more in addition,
not if Priam son of Dardanos should offer to
weigh out your bulk in gold; not even so shall the lady your
     mother
who herself bore you lay you on the death-bed and mourn you: 115
no, but the dogs and the birds will have you all for their
     feasting."
     Then, dying, Hektor of the shining helmet spoke to him:
"I know you well as I look upon you, I know that I could not
persuade you, since indeed in your breast is a heart of iron.
Be careful now; for I might be made into the gods' curse   120
upon you, on that day when Paris and Phoibos Apollo
destroy you in the Skaian gates, for all your valor."
     He spoke, and as he spoke the end of death closed in upon him,
and the soul fluttering free of the limbs went down into Death's
     house
mourning her destiny, leaving youth and manhood behind her.   125
Now though he was a dead man brilliant Achilleus spoke to
     him:
"Die: and I will take my own death at whatever time
Zeus and the rest of the immortals choose to accomplish it."

Dardanos: a son of Zeus and ancestor of Hektor
Paris: Hektor's brother
Phoibos Apollo: Greek god of light and the sun
Skaian gates: the southern gates into the city of Troy

THE
CANTERBURY
TALES

from THE PROLOGUE

Geoffrey Chaucer, translated by Nevill Coghill

Geoffrey Chaucer (c. 1343–1400) chose to write his poetry not in French, the official language of the English court, nor in Latin, the official language of the church, but in the vernacular — the everyday language — of his time and place. That vernacular was a form of English that scholars now call Middle English. Chaucer's masterpiece, The Canterbury Tales, *is a collection of stories in verse. Chaucer uses the device of a frame story — a story that includes other stories. The frame describes a pilgrimage, a religious journey, in which a group is on its way to Canterbury Cathedral.* The Canterbury Tales *opens with a General Prologue that introduces the pilgrims, a diverse group including a knight, a miller, a prioress, a carpenter, a merchant, and Chaucer himself. The group decides to exchange stories as a way of passing time during their journey. Many of the stories are vivid retellings of old tales. What is most remarkable, however, is Chaucer's achievement in portraying each storyteller as a distinct individual, each with his or her own particular motivations, traits, and foibles. Presenting figures from a range of medieval society — including the church, the court, and the emerging middle class — Chaucer's remarkably diverse and individualized characterizations constitute what one scholar has called "a concise portrait of an entire nation, high and low, old and young, male and female, lay and clerical learned and ignorant, rogue and righteous."*

When in April the sweet showers fall
And pierce the drought of March to the root, and all
The veins are bathed in liquor of such power
As brings about the engendering of the flower,
When also Zephyrus with his sweet breath   5
Exhales an air in every grove and heath

---

engendering: blooming
Zephyrus: in Greek mythology, the god of the west wind
heath: uncultivated land

Upon the tender shoots, and the young sun
His half-course in the sign of the *Ram* has run,
And the small fowl are making melody
That sleep away the night with open eye   10
(So nature pricks them and their heart engages)
Then people long to go on pilgrimages
And palmers long to seek the stranger strands
Of far-off saints, hallowed in sundry lands,
And specially, from every shire's end   15
Of England, down to Canterbury they wend
To seek the holy blissful martyr, quick
To give his help to them when they were sick.
    It happened in that season that one day
In Southwark, at *The Tabard*, as I lay   20
Ready to go on pilgrimage and start
For Canterbury, most devout at heart,
At night there came into that hostelry
Some nine and twenty in a company
Of sundry folk happening then to fall   25
In fellowship, and they were pilgrims all
That towards Canterbury meant to ride.
The rooms and stables of the inn were wide:
They made us easy, all was of the best.
And, briefly, when the sun had gone to rest,   30
I'd spoken to them all upon the trip

---

the sign of the *Ram*: in the zodiac calendar, the month devoted to
    Aries, which runs from mid-March to mid-April
pilgrimages: trips to religiously significant places
palmers: pilgrims who have traveled to the Holy Land
strands: beaches
shire: the medieval equivalent of a county
Canterbury: a town in southeast England and a popular destination
    for medieval pilgrims
wend: go; travel
martyr: one who had died for his or her religious beliefs; in this
    case, St. Thomas Becket, a twelfth-century archbishop of
    Canterbury
Southwark: a part of London directly south of the River Thames (in
    Chaucer's time, it was outside of the city's boundaries)
hostelry: inn

And was soon one with them in fellowship,
Pledged to rise early and to take the way
To Canterbury, as you heard me say.
    But none the less, while I have time and space,   35
Before my story takes a further pace,
It seems a reasonable thing to say
What their condition was, the full array
Of each of them, as it appeared to me,
According to profession and degree,   40
And what apparel they were riding in;
And at a Knight I therefore will begin.
There was a *Knight*, a most distinguished man,
Who from the day on which he first began
To ride abroad had followed chivalry,   45
Truth, honor, generousness, and courtesy.
He had done nobly in his sovereign's war
And ridden into battle, no man more,
As well in Christian as in heathen places,
And ever honored for his noble graces.   50
    When we took Alexandria, he was there.
He often sat at table in the chair
Of honor, above all nations, when in Prussia.
In Lithuania he had ridden, and Russia,
No Christian man so often, of his rank.   55
When, in Granada, Algeciras sank
Under assault, he had been there, and in
North Africa, raiding Benamarin;

---

array: collection
chivalry: medieval code of conduct practiced by knights
sovereign's: king's; monarch's
heathen: in this context, non-Christian
Alexandria: a city in Egypt
Prussia: a former kingdom in Europe occupying parts of what is
    now Germany and Poland
Lithuania: a region in eastern Europe
Granada: a city in southern Spain
Algeciras sank / Under assault: the overtaking of a southern
    Spanish city by the Moors in the mid-fourteenth century
Benmarin: a region in Morocco

In Anatolia he had been as well
And fought when Ayas and Attalia fell,   60
For all along the Mediterranean coast
He had embarked with many a noble host.
In fifteen mortal battles he had been
And jousted for our faith at Tramissene
Thrice in the lists, and always killed his man.   65
This same distinguished knight had led the van
Once with the Bey of Balat, doing work
For him against another heathen Turk;
He was of sovereign value in all eyes.
And though so much distinguished, he was wise   70
And in his bearing modest as a maid.
He never yet a boorish thing had said
In all his life to any, come what might;
He was a true, a perfect gentle-knight.

    Speaking of his equipment, he possessed   75
Fine horses, but he was not gaily dressed.
He wore a fustian tunic stained and dark
With smudges where his armor had left mark;
Just home from service, he had joined our ranks
To do his pilgrimage and render thanks.   80

    He had his son with him, a fine young *Squire*,
A lover and cadet, a lad of fire
With locks as curly as if they had been pressed.
He was some twenty years of age, I guessed.
In stature he was of a moderate length,   85
With wonderful agility and strength.
He'd seen some service with the cavalry

Anatolia: a region in modern-day Turkey
Ayas: a region in southern France
Attalia: a city on the Mediterranean Sea in what is now Turkey
Tramissene: a town in northwest Algeria
Bey of Balat: a bay of Istanbul, Turkey
boorish: crude
a fustian tunic: a robe of strong cotton
Squire: a knight's attendant

In Flanders and Artois and Picardy
And had done valiantly in little space
Of time, in hope to win his lady's grace.   90
He was embroidered like a meadow bright
And full of freshest flowers, red and white.
Singing he was, or fluting all the day;
He was as fresh as is the month of May.
Short was his gown, the sleeves were long and   95
    wide;
He knew the way to sit a horse and ride.
He could make songs and poems and recite,
Knew how to joust and dance, to draw and write.
He loved so hotly that till dawn grew pale
He slept as little as a nightingale.   100
Courteous he was, lowly and serviceable,
And carved to serve his father at the table.
    There was a *Yeoman* with him at his side,
No other servant; so he chose to ride.
This Yeoman wore a coat and hood of green,   105
And peacock-feathered arrows, bright and keen
And neatly sheathed, hung at his belt the while
— For he could dress his gear in yeoman style,
His arrows never drooped their feathers low —
And in his hand he bore a mighty bow.   110
His head was like a nut, his face was brown.
He knew the whole of woodcraft up and down.
A saucy brace was on his arm to ward
It from the bow-string, and a shield and sword
Hung at one side, and at the other slipped   115
A jaunty dirk, spear-sharp and well-equipped.
A medal of St. Christopher he wore

Flanders: a medieval kingdom occupying what is now northern
    France and Belgium and part of southern Holland
Artois: a province of northern France close to the English Channel
Picardy: a province of northern France that borders Artois
Yeoman: a farmer who owns his own land
dirk: sharp dagger
St. Christopher: Saint Christopher, patron saint of travelers

Of shining silver on his breast, and bore
A hunting-horn, well slung and burnished clean,
That dangled from a baldrick of bright green.   120
He was a proper forester, I guess.
    There also was a *Nun*, a Prioress,
Her way of smiling very simple and coy.
Her greatest oath was only "By St. Loy!"
And she was known as Madam Eglantyne.   125
And well she sang a service, with a fine
Intoning through her nose, as was most seemly,
And she spoke daintily in French, extremely,
After the school of Stratford-atte-Bowe;
French in the Paris style she did not know.   130
At meat her manners were well taught withal;
No morsel from her lips did she let fall,
Nor dipped her fingers in the sauce too deep;
But she could carry a morsel up and keep
The smallest drop from falling on her breast.   135
For courtliness she had a special zest,
And she would wipe her upper lip so clean
That not a trace of grease was to be seen
Upon the cup when she had drunk; to eat,
She reached a hand sedately for the meat.   140
She certainly was very entertaining,
Pleasant and friendly in her ways, and straining
To counterfeit a courtly kind of grace,
A stately bearing fitting to her place,
And to seem dignified in all her dealings.   145
As for her sympathies and tender feelings,
She was so charitably solicitous

---

baldrick: a belt worn over the shoulder and often used to carry a
    weapon or an instrument
forester: one with knowledge of the forests and a proficient hunter
Prioress: the head of a nunnery; a mother superior
intoning: chanting or singing
Stratford-atte-Bow: an area of East London
at meat: during mealtimes
withal: nonetheless
courtliness: good manners

She used to weep if she but saw a mouse
Caught in a trap, if it were dead or bleeding.
And she had little dogs she would be feeding   150
With roasted flesh, or milk, or fine white bread.
And bitterly she wept if one were dead
Or someone took a stick and made it smart;
She was all sentiment and tender heart.
Her veil was gathered in a seemly way,   155
Her nose was elegant, her eyes glass-gray;
Her mouth was very small, but soft and red,
Her forehead, certainly, was fair of spread,
Almost a span across the brows, I own;
She was indeed by no means undergrown.   160
Her cloak, I noticed, had a graceful charm.
She wore a coral trinket on her arm,
A set of beads, the gaudies tricked in green,
Whence hung a golden brooch of brightest sheen
On which there first was graven a crowned A,   165
And lower, *Amor vincit omnia.*
 Another *Nun*, the secretary at her cell,
Was riding with her, and *three Priests* as well.
 A *Monk* there was, one of the finest sort
Who rode the country; hunting was his sport.   170
A manly man, to be an Abbott able;
Many a dainty horse he had in stable.
His bridle, when he rode, a man might hear
Jingling in a whistling wind as clear,
Aye, and as loud as does the chapel bell   175
Where my lord Monk was Prior of the cell.

---

span: nine inches
gaudies: large beads in a rosary, marking the time for the Lord's
    Prayer
Amor vincit omnia: Latin for "Love conquers all"
Abbott: the superior ranking member of a monastery
Prior: after the abbot, the next-highest ranking member of a
    monastery

The Rule of good St. Benet or St. Maur
As old and strict he tended to ignore;
He let go by the things of yesterday
And took the modern world's more spacious way.   180
He did not rate that text at a plucked hen
Which says that hunters are not holy men
And that a monk uncloistered is a mere
Fish out of water, flapping on the pier,
That is to say a monk out of his cloister.   185
That was a text he held not worth an oyster;
And I agreed and said his views were sound;
Was he to study till his head went round
Poring over books in cloisters? Must he toil
As Austin bade and till the very soil?   190
Was he to leave the world upon the shelf?
Let Austin have his labor to himself.

    This Monk was therefore a good man to horse;
Greyhounds he had, as swift as birds, to course.
Hunting a hare or riding at a fence   195
Was all his fun, he spared for no expense.
I saw his sleeves were garnished at the hand
With fine gray fur, the finest in the land,
And on his hood, to fasten it at his chin
He had a wrought-gold, cunningly fashioned pin;   200
Into a lover's knot it seemed to pass.
His head was bald and shone like looking-glass;
So did his face, as if it had been greased.
He was a fat and personable priest;
His prominent eyeballs never seemed to settle.   205

St. Benet: Saint Benedict, a fifth-century monk who wrote a set of
    rules for monastic life
St. Maur: a disciple of St. Benedict
did not rate…a plucked hen: paid no attention to the idea
uncloistered: outside of a secluded residence for religiously devout
    individuals
Austin: St. Augustine, the bishop of Hippo, taught that monks
    should do physical work in addition to spending their lives in
    contemplation and prayer
course: to command to hunt

They glittered like the flames beneath a kettle;
Supple his boots, his horse in fine condition.
He was a prelate fit for exhibition,
He was not pale like a tormented soul.
He liked a fat swan best, and roasted whole. 210
His palfrey was as brown as is a berry.
    There was a *Friar*, a wanton one and merry,
A Limiter, a very festive fellow.
In all Four Orders there was none so mellow,
So glib with gallant phrase and well-turned speech. 215
He'd fixed up many a marriage, giving each
Of his young women what he could afford her.
He was a noble pillar to his Order.
Highly beloved and intimate was he
With County folk within his boundary, 220
And city dames of honor and possessions;
For he was qualified to hear confessions,
Or so he said, with more than priestly scope;
He had a special license from the Pope.
Sweetly he heard his penitents at shrift 225
With pleasant absolution, for a gift.
He was an easy man in penance-giving
Where he could hope to make a decent living;
It's a sure sign whenever gifts are given
To a poor Order that a man's well shriven, 230

---

prelate: a high-ranking priest or clergy member
palfrey: a riding horse
Friar: a monk who has given up all possessions
wanton: used here to mean "carefree"
Limiter: a monk with the right to ask for gifts on which to live and
    to preach in a limited area
Four Orders: four orders of friars, which are the Franciscans,
    Dominicans, Carmelites, and Augustinians
pillar: a prominent supporter or member
penitents: people seeking absolution or forgiveness for their sins
shrift: in the Catholic Church, the hearing of confessions
absolution: forgiveness; pardon
penance: deeds or prayers required by the church to atone for past
    sins
shriven: pardoned for one's sins

And should he give enough he knew in verity
The penitent repented in sincerity.
For many a fellow is so hard of heart
He cannot weep, for all his inward smart.
Therefore instead of weeping and of prayer   235
One should give silver for a poor Friar's care.
He kept his tippet stuffed with pins for curls,
And pocket-knives, to give to pretty girls.
And certainly his voice was gay and sturdy,
For he sang well and played the hurdy-gurdy.   240
At sing-songs he was champion of the hour.
His neck was whiter than a lily-flower
But strong enough to butt a bruiser down.
He knew the taverns well in every town
And every innkeeper and barmaid too   245
Better than lepers, beggars and that crew,
For in so eminent a man as he
It was not fitting with the dignity
Of his position, dealing with a scum
Of wretched lepers; nothing good can come   250
Of commerce with such slum-and-gutter dwellers,
But only with the rich and victual-sellers.
But anywhere a profit might accrue
Courteous he was and lowly of service too.
Natural gifts like his were hard to match.   255
He was the finest beggar of his batch,
And, for his begging-district, paid a rent;
His brethren did no poaching where he went.
For though a widow mightn't have a shoe,
So pleasant was his holy how-d'ye-do   260
He got his farthing from her just the same

---

verity: truth
tippet: a broad scarf worn by priests
hurdy-gurdy: a medieval stringed instrument played by turning a
    handle
eminent: important
victual: food
farthing: a low-value coin

Before he left, and so his income came
To more than he laid out. And how he romped,
Just like a puppy! He was ever prompt
To arbitrate disputes on settling days   265
(For a small fee) in many helpful ways,
Not then appearing as your cloistered scholar
With threadbare habit hardly worth a dollar,
But much more like a Doctor or a Pope.
Of double-worsted was the semi-cope   270
Upon his shoulders, and the swelling fold
About him, like a bell about its mould
When it is casting, rounded out his dress.
He lisped a little out of wantonness
To make his English sweet upon his tongue.   275
When he had played his harp, or having sung,
His eyes would twinkle in his head as bright
As any star upon a frosty night.
This worthy's name was Hubert, it appeared.

    There was a *Merchant* with a forking beard   280
And motley dress; high on his horse he sat,
Upon his head a Flemish beaver hat
And on his feet daintily buckled boots.
He told of his opinions and pursuits
In solemn tones, he harped on his increase   285
Of capital; there should be sea-police
(He thought) upon the Harwich-Holland ranges;
He was expert at dabbling in exchanges.
This estimable Merchant so had set
His wits to work, none knew he was in debt,   290
He was so stately in administration,

---

arbitrate: settle
threadbare: thin
worsted: a tightly woven woolen fabric
semi-cope: a cloak worn by clergy
motley: multicolored clothes, suggesting his wealth
Flemish: originating in northern and western Belgium
Harwich-Holland ranges: routes between England and the
    Netherlands
estimable: worthy

In loans and bargains and negotiation.
He was an excellent fellow all the same;
To tell the truth I do not know his name.
    An *Oxford Cleric*, still a student though,   295
One who had taken logic long ago,
Was there; his horse was thinner than a rake,
And he was not too fat, I undertake,
But had a hollow look, a sober stare;
The thread upon his overcoat was bare.   300
He had found no preferment in the church
And he was too unworldly to make search
For secular employment. By his bed
He preferred having twenty books in red
And black, of Aristotle's philosophy,   305
Than costly clothes, fiddle, or psaltery.
Though a philosopher, as I have told,
He had not found the stone for making gold.
Whatever money from his friends he took
He spent on learning or another book   310
And prayed for them most earnestly, returning
Thanks to them thus for paying for his learning.
His only care was study, and indeed
He never spoke a word more than was need,
Formal at that, respectful in the extreme,   315
Short, to the point, and lofty in his theme.
A tone of moral virtue filled his speech
And gladly would he learn, and gladly teach.
    A *Serjeant at the Law* who paid his calls,
Wary and wise, for clients at St. Paul's   320

Cleric: a member of the clergy who can read and write
preferment: advancement or payment in money or land
unworldly: reclusive and studious; not secular
secular: relating to the state, as opposed to the church
Aristotle: an important ancient Greek philosopher
psaltery: a stringed instrument in the harp family
Serjeant at the Law: a lawyer
St. Paul's: Saint Paul's Cathedral; a prominent church in London,
    outside of which lawyers congregated when the courts were
    closed

There also was, of noted excellence.
Discreet he was, a man to reverence,
Or so he seemed, his sayings were so wise.
He often had been Justice of Assize
By letters patent, and in full commission.   325
His fame and learning and his high position
Had won him many a robe and many a fee.
There was no such conveyancer as he;
All was fee-simple to his strong digestion,
Not one conveyance could be called in question.   330
Though there was nowhere one so busy as he,
He was less busy than he seemed to be.
He knew of every judgment, case, and crime
Ever recorded since King William's time.
He could dictate defenses or draft deeds;   335
No one could pinch a comma from his screeds
And he knew every statute off by rote.
He wore a homely parti-colored coat,
Girt with a silken belt of pin-stripe stuff;
Of his appearance I have said enough.   340
    There was a *Franklin* with him, it appeared;
White as a daisy-petal was his beard.
A sanguine man, high-colored and benign,
He loved a morning sop of cake in wine.
He lived for pleasure and had always done,   345
For he was Epicurus' very son,

---

discreet: tactful; diplomatic
Justice of Assize: a judge in a jury trial
conveyancer: a lawyer involved in the buying and selling of
    property or drawing up a deed
fee-simple: absolute title or ownership to land
King William: William the Conqueror, king of England from 1066
    to 1087
screeds: lengthy writings
Franklin: prosperous land owner
sanguine: rosy skinned, thought to be a sign of a cheerful
    disposition
benign: kind
Epicurus: an ancient Greek philosopher whose teachings
    maintained that the purpose of life was to pursue pleasure

In whose opinion sensual delight
Was the one true felicity in sight.
As noted as St. Julian was for bounty
He made his household free to all the County.   350
His bread, his ale were finest of the fine
And no one had a better stock of wine.
His house was never short of bake-meat pies,
Of fish and flesh, and these in such supplies
It positively snowed with meat and drink   355
And all the dainties that a man could think.
According to the seasons of the year
Changes of dish were ordered to appear.
He kept fat partridges in coops, beyond,
Many a bream and pike were in his pond.   360
Woe to the cook unless the sauce was hot
And sharp, or if he wasn't on the spot!
And in his hall a table stood arrayed
And ready all day long, with places laid.
As Justice at the Sessions none stood higher;   365
He often had been Member for the Shire.
A dagger and a little purse of silk
Hung at his girdle, white as morning milk.
As Sheriff he checked audit, every entry.
He was a model among landed gentry.   370

   A *Haberdasher*, a *Dyer*, a *Carpenter*,
A *Weaver*, and a *Carpet-maker* were
Among our ranks, all in the livery

St. Julian: also known as Julian the Hospitaller, a Catholic saint
    who was legendary for his hospitality and kind treatment of
    travelers
bream and pike: types of fish
Member: a member of Parliament, England's national legislative
    assembly
audit: account
landed gentry: members of the aristocracy who owned land
Haberdasher: one who makes and sells men's clothes and
    furnishings such as buttons
livery: clothes

Of one impressive guild-fraternity.
They were so trim and fresh their gear would pass   375
For new. Their knives were not tricked out with
    brass
But wrought with purest silver, which avouches
A like display on girdles and on pouches.
Each seemed a worthy burgess, fit to grace
A guild-hall with a seat upon the dais.   380
Their wisdom would have justified a plan
To make each one of them an alderman;
They had the capital and revenue,
Besides their wives declared it was their due.
And if they did not think so, then they ought;   385
To be called *"Madam"* is a glorious thought,
And so is going to church and being seen
Having your mantle carried, like a queen.
    They had a *Cook* with them who stood alone
For boiling chicken with a marrow-bone,   390
Sharp flavoring-powder and a spice for savor.
He could distinguish London ale by flavor,
And he could roast and seethe and broil and fry,
Make good thick soup, and bake a tasty pie.
But what a pity—so it seemed to me,   395
That he should have an ulcer on his knee.
As for blancmange, he made it with the best.
    There was a *Skipper* hailing from far west;
He came from Dartmouth, so I understood.

---

guild: an association of craftsmen
avouches: declares
burgess: a free citizen of a town or borough
guild-hall: a building for public business, often the seat of local
    government; a town or city hall
dais: head table
alderman: a representative in local government; head of a guild
mantle: a ceremonial cloak that signifies importance or authority
marrow-bone: a bone that is used to flavor soup
ulcer: an open sore
blancmange: a dessert often flavored with almonds
Skipper: a sailor
Dartmouth: a port town in Devon, southwest England

He rode a farmer's horse as best he could,   400
In a woollen gown that reached his knee.
A dagger on a lanyard falling free
Hung from his neck under his arm and down.
The summer heat had tanned his color brown,
And certainly he was an excellent fellow.   405
Many a draught of vintage, red and yellow,
He'd drawn at Bordeaux, while the trader snored.
The nicer rules of conscience he ignored.
If, when he fought, the enemy vessel sank,
He sent his prisoners home; they walked the plank. 410
As for his skill in reckoning his tides,
Currents, and many another risk besides,
Moons, harbors, pilots, he had such dispatch
That none from Hull to Carthage was his match.
Hardy he was, prudent in undertaking;   415
His beard in many a tempest had its shaking,
And he knew all the havens as they were
From Gottland to the Cape of Finisterre,
And every creek in Brittany and Spain;
The barge he owned was called *The Maudelayne*.   420

    A *Doctor* too emerged as we proceeded;
No one alive could talk as well as he did
On points of medicine and of surgery,
For, being grounded in astronomy,
He watched his patient closely for the hours   425
When, by his horoscope, he knew the powers
Of favorable planets, then ascendent,
Worked on the images for his dependent.

---

lanyard: a strap
Bordeaux: a region in France known for its wine
from Hull to Carthage: from towns in England to towns in Spain
tempest: storm
havens: safe ports
Gottland: a province in Sweden
Cape of Finisterre: a cape on the western coast of Spain
Brittany: a medieval kingdom located in what is now northwestern
    France
ascendent: in a position to have dominating influence

The cause of every malady you'd got
He knew, and whether dry, cold, moist, or hot;   430
He knew their seat, their humor and condition.
He was a perfect practicing physician.
These causes being known for what they were,
He gave the man his medicine then and there.
All his apothecaries in a tribe   435
Were ready with the drugs he would prescribe
And each made money from the other's guile;
They had been friendly for a goodish while.
He was well-versed in Aesculapius too
And what Hippocrates and Rufus knew   440
And Dioscorides, now dead and gone,
Galen and Rhazes, Hali, Serapion,
Averroes, Avicenna, Constantine,
Scotch Bernard, John of Gaddesden, Gilbertine.
In his own diet he observed some measure;   445
There were no superfluities for pleasure,
Only digestives, nutritives and such.
He did not read the Bible very much.
In blood-red garments, slashed with bluish gray
And lined with taffeta, he rode his way;   450
Yet he was rather close as to expenses
And kept the gold he won in pestilences.
Gold stimulates the heart, or so we're told.
He therefore had a special love of gold.
     A worthy *woman* from beside *Bath* city   455

---

malady: sickness
humor: one of four fluids in the body, the balance or imbalance
    of which was thought by medieval doctors to be the cause of
    human diseases
apothecaries: pharmacists
guile: deceit
Aesculapius…Gilbertine: important and influential doctors
    throughout history from the times of the ancient Greeks to the
    medieval period in England
superfluities: unnecessary or unessential things
taffeta: a smooth, silky fabric
pestilences: diseases
Bath: a town west of London

Was with us, somewhat deaf, which was a pity.
In making cloth she showed so great a bent
She bettered those of Ypres and of Ghent.
In all the parish not a dame dared stir
Towards the altar steps in front of her,   460
And if indeed they did, so wrath was she
As to be quite put out of charity.
Her kerchiefs were of finely woven ground;
I dared have sworn they weighed a good ten pound,
The ones she wore on Sunday, on her head.   465
Her hose were of the finest scarlet red
And gartered tight; her shoes were soft and new.
Bold was her face, handsome, and red in hue.
A worthy woman all her life, what's more
She'd had five husbands, all at the church door,   470
Apart from other company in youth;
No need just now to speak of that, forsooth.
And she had thrice been to Jerusalem,
Seen many strange rivers and passed over them;
She'd been to Rome and also to Boulogne,   475
St. James of Compostella and Cologne,
And she was skilled in wandering by the way.
She had gap-teeth, set widely, truth to say.
Easily on an ambling horse she sat
Well wimpled up, and on her head a hat   480
As broad as is a buckler or a shield;
She had a flowing mantle that concealed
Large hips, her heels spurred sharply under that.
In company she liked to laugh and chat

---

bent: talent
of Ypres and of Ghent: relating to two Belgian towns famous for the
    clothing made there
gartered: tied
Boulogne, St. James of Compostella, and Cologne: popular
    destinations for medieval pilgrimages
ambling: walking at a leisurely pace
well wimpled up: her head well covered
buckler: a type of shield worn on one's forearm
mantle: a long skirt worn by women when riding horses

And knew the remedies for love's mischances,   485
An art in which she knew the oldest dances.
        A holy-minded man of good renown
There was, and poor, the *Parson* to a town,
Yet he was rich in holy thought and work.
He also was a learned man, a clerk,   490
Who truly knew Christ's gospel and would
        preach it
Devoutly to parishioners, and teach it.
Benign and wonderfully diligent,
And patient when adversity was sent
(For so he proved in much adversity)   495
He hated cursing to extort a fee,
Nay rather he preferred beyond a doubt
Giving to poor parishioners round about
Both from church offerings and his property;
He could in little find sufficiency.   500
Wide was his parish, with houses far asunder,
Yet he neglected not in rain or thunder,
In sickness or in grief, to pay a call
On the remotest, whether great or small,
Upon his feet, and in his hand a stave.   505
This noble example to his sheep he gave
That first he wrought, and afterward he taught;
And it was from the Gospel he had caught
Those words, and he would add this figure too,
That if gold rust, what then will iron do?   510
For if a priest be foul in whom we trust
No wonder that a common man should rust;
And shame it is to see—let priests take stock—
A shitten shepherd and a snowy flock.
The true example that a priest should give   515
Is one of cleanness, how the sheep should live.

Parson: a priest of a small church
extort: to threaten with excommunication
far asunder: spread far apart
stave: a staff

He did not set his benefice to hire
And leave his sheep encumbered in the mire
Or run to London to earn easy bread
By singing masses for the wealthy dead, 520
Or find some Brotherhood and get enrolled.
He stayed at home and watched over his fold
So that no wolf should make the sheep miscarry.
He was a shepherd and no mercenary.
Holy and virtuous he was, but then 525
Never contemptuous of sinful men,
Never disdainful, never too proud or fine,
But was discreet in teaching and benign.
His business was to show a fair behavior
And draw men thus to Heaven and their Savior, 530
Unless indeed a man were obstinate;
And such, whether of high or low estate,
He put to sharp rebuke, to say the least.
I think there never was a better priest.
He sought no pomp or glory in his dealings, 535
No scrupulosity had spiced his feelings.
Christ and His Twelve Apostles and their lore
He taught, but followed it himself before.

There was a *Plowman* with him there, his brother;
Many a load of dung one time or other 540
He must have carted through the morning dew.
He was an honest worker, good and true,
Living in peace and perfect charity,
And, as the gospel bade him, so did he,

---

benefice to hire: hire someone else to do the blessings
encumbered: overburdened
mire: mud and muck
find some Brotherhood: become a paid chaplain for a guild
fold: a flock; an enclosure for sheep
mercenary: one whose actions are for profit or personal gain alone
contemptuous: disdainful
obstinate: unreasonably stubborn
rebuke: reprimand; criticism
pomp: spectacle; empty ceremony
scrupulosity: having strictest concern for what is proper

Loving God best with all his heart and mind 545
And then his neighbor as himself, repined
At no misfortune, slacked for no content,
For steadily about his work he went
To thrash his corn, to dig or to manure
Or make a ditch; and he would help the poor 550
For love of Christ and never take a penny
If he could help it, and, as prompt as any,
He paid his tithes in full when they were due
On what he owned, and on his earnings too.
He wore a tabard smock and rode a mare. 555
    There was a *Reeve,* also a *Miller,* there,
A College *Manciple* from the Inns of Court,
A papal *Pardoner* and, in close consort,
A Church-Court *Summoner,* riding at a trot,
And finally myself—that was the lot. 560
    The *Miller* was a chap of sixteen stone,
A great stout fellow big in brawn and bone.
He did well out of them, for he could go
And win the ram at any wrestling show.
Broad, knotty, and short-shouldered, he 565
    would boast
He could heave any door off hinge and post,
Or take a run and break it with his head.
His beard, like any sow or fox, was red
And broad as well, as though it were a spade;
And, at its very tip, his nose displayed 570

---

repined: complained
thrash: to separate grain from its stalk by beating it
tithes: payments due to the church
tabard: a sleeveless tunic
a Reeve…a Miller…/ a College Manciple…/ a papal Pardoner…/ a
    Church-Court Summoner: in order, one elected to supervise
    a landlord's property; one who operates a grain mill; one
    who managed the food supplies at a monastery, university,
    law court, or other such institution; a clergyman who sold
    pardons to people for sins they committed; one who summoned
    individuals to church courts for allegedly sinful behavior
sixteen stone: 224 pounds (one stone is 14 pounds)
spade: a flat, broad shovel

A wart on which there stood a tuft of hair
Red as the bristles in an old sow's ear.
His nostrils were as black as they were wide.
He had a sword and buckler at his side,
His mighty mouth was like a furnace door. 575
A wrangler and buffoon, he had a store
Of tavern stories, filthy in the main.
His was a master-hand at stealing grain.
He felt it with his thumb and thus he knew
Its quality and took three times his due— 580
A thumb of gold, by God, to gauge an oat!
He wore a hood of blue and a white coat.
He liked to play his bagpipes up and down
And that was how he brought us out of town.

The *Manciple* came from the Inner Temple; 585
All caterers might follow his example
In buying victuals; he was never rash
Whether he bought on credit or paid cash.
He used to watch the market most precisely
And got in first, and so he did quite nicely. 590
Now isn't it a marvel of God's grace
That an illiterate fellow can outpace
The wisdom of a heap of learned men?
His masters—he had more than thirty then—
All versed in the abstrusest legal knowledge, 595
Could have produced a dozen from their College
Fit to be stewards in land and rents and game
To any Peer in England you could name,
And show him how to live on what he had
Debt-free (unless of course the Peer were mad) 600
Or be as frugal as he might desire,
And make them fit to help about the Shire
In any legal case there was to try;

wrangler: a person who tells bawdy stories
Inner Temple: one of England's four courts of law
abstrusest: most obscure
stewards: caretakers
Peer: nobleman

And yet this Manciple could wipe their eye.
    The *Reeve* was old and choleric and thin;   605
His beard was shaven closely to the skin,
His shorn hair came abruptly to a stop
Above his ears, and he was docked on top
Just like a priest in front; his legs were lean,
Like sticks they were, no calf was to be seen.   610
He kept his bins and garners very trim;
No auditor could gain a point on him.
And he could judge by watching drought and rain
The yield he might expect from seed and grain.
His master's sheep, his animals and hens,   615
Pigs, horses, dairies, stores, and cattle-pens
Were wholly trusted to his government.
He had been under contract to present
The accounts, right from his master's earliest years.
No one had ever caught him in arrears.   620
No bailiff, serf, or herdsman dared to kick,
He knew their dodges, knew their every trick;
Feared like the plague he was, by those beneath.
He had a lovely dwelling on a heath,
Shadowed in green by trees above the sward.   625
A better hand at bargains than his lord,
He had grown rich and had a store of treasure
Well tucked away, yet out it came to pleasure
His lord with subtle loans or gifts of goods,
To earn his thanks and even coats and hoods.   630
When young he'd learnt a useful trade and still
He was a carpenter of first-rate skill.
The stallion-cob he rode at a slow trot
Was dapple-gray and bore the name of Scot.
He wore an overcoat of bluish shade   635
And rather long; he had a rusty blade
Slung at his side. He came, as I heard tell,

---

choleric: hot-tempered
bins and garners: places where grain is stored
in arrears: in debt
sward: grassy ground; lawn

40

From Norfolk, near a place called Baldeswell.
His coat was tucked under his belt and splayed.
He rode the hindmost of our cavalcade.   640
　　　There was a *Summoner* with us at that Inn,
His face on fire, like a cherubim,
For he had carbuncles. His eyes were narrow,
He was as hot and lecherous as a sparrow.
Black scabby brows he had, and a thin beard.   645
Children were afraid when he appeared.
No quicksilver, lead ointment, tartar creams,
No brimstone, no boracic, so it seems,
Could make a salve that had the power to bite,
Clean up, or cure his whelks of knobby white   650
Or purge the pimples sitting on his cheeks.
Garlic he loved, and onions too, and leeks,
And drinking strong red wine till all was hazy.
Then he would shout and jabber as if crazy,
And wouldn't speak a word except in Latin   655
When he was drunk, such tags as he was pat in;
He only had a few, say two or three,
That he had mugged up out of some decree;
No wonder, for he heard them every day.
And, as you know, a man can teach a jay   660
To call out "Walter" better than the Pope.
But had you tried to test his wits and grope
For more, you'd have found nothing in the bag.
Then *"Questio quid juris"* was his tag.
He was a noble varlet and a kind one,   665

Norfolk: a county in eastern England
cavalcade: procession of horses
cherubim: child-angels with rosy cheeks
carbuncles: boils; pustules
lecherous: immoral; lusty
quicksilver, lead ointment tartar creams /…brimstone…boracic:
　　　cleansing agents and disinfectants during medieval times
salve: balm; healing cream
whelks: sores filled with pus
Questio quid juris: Latin for "I ask what point of the law?"
varlet: a rogue or a scoundrel

You'd meet none better if you went to find one.
Why, he'd allow—just for a quart of wine—
Any good lad to keep a concubine
A twelvemonth and dispense him altogether!
And he had finches of his own to feather: 670
And if he found some rascal with a maid
He would instruct him not to be afraid
In such a case of the Archdeacon's curse
(Unless the rascal's soul were in his purse)
For in his purse the punishment should be.   675
"Purse is the good Archdeacon's Hell," said he.
But well I know he lied in what he said;
A curse should put a guilty man in dread,
For curses kill, as shriving brings, salvation.
We should beware of excommunication.   680
Thus, as he pleased, the man could bring duress
On any young fellow in the diocese.
He knew their secrets, they did what he said.
He wore a garland set upon his head
Large as the holly-bush upon a stake   685
Outside an ale-house, and he had a cake,
A round one, which it was his joke to wield
As if it were intended for a shield.

    He and a gentle *Pardoner* rode together,
A bird from Charing Cross of the same feather,   690
Just back from visiting the Court of Rome.
He loudly sang *"Come hither, love, come home!"*
The Summoner sang deep seconds to this song,
No trumpet ever sounded half so strong.
This Pardoner had hair as yellow as wax,   695
Hanging down smoothly like a hank of flax.

---

finches of his own to feather: *to feather a finch* is an idiom meaning
    "to swindle someone"
Archdeacon: a high-ranking member of the clergy
duress: pressure
diocese: a geographical region administered by a bishop
Charing Cross: an area in London
seconds: harmonies
a hank of flax: a clump of flax, a pale-colored plant fiber

In driblets fell his locks behind his head
Down to his shoulders which they overspread;
Thinly they fell, like rat-tails, one by one.
He wore no hood upon his head, for fun;   700
The hood inside his wallet had been stowed,
He aimed at riding in the latest mode;
But for a little cap his head was bare
And he had bulging eye-balls, like a hare.
He'd sewed a holy relic on his cap;   705
His wallet lay before him on his lap,
Brimful of pardons come from Rome, all hot.
He had the same small voice a goat has got.
His chin no beard had harbored, nor would harbor,
Smoother than ever chin was left by barber.   710
I judge he was a gelding, or a mare.
As to his trade, from Berwick down to Ware
There was no pardoner of equal grace,
For in his trunk he had a pillow-case
Which he asserted was Our Lady's veil.   715
He said he had a gobbet of the sail
Saint Peter had the time when he made bold
To walk the waves, till Jesu Christ took hold.
He had a cross of metal set with stones
And, in a glass, a rubble of pigs' bones.   720
And with these relics, any time he found
Some poor up-country parson to astound,
In one short day, in money down, he drew
More than the parson in a month or two,
And by his flatteries and prevarication   725
Made monkeys of the priest and congregation.
But still to do him justice first and last
In church he was a noble ecclesiast.
How well he read a lesson or told a story!

Berwick down to Ware: between two distant towns in England
Our Lady: the Virgin Mary
gobbet: small piece
prevarication: lies
ecclesiast: member of the church

But best of all he sang an Offertory, 730
For well he knew that when that song was sung
He'd have to preach and tune his honey-tongue
And (well he could) win silver from the crowd.
That's why he sang so merrily and loud.

Now I have told you shortly, in a clause, 735
The rank, the array, the number, and the cause
Of our assembly in this company
In Southwark, at that high-class hostelry
Known as *The Tabard*, close beside *The Bell*.
And now the time has come for me to tell 740
How we behaved that evening; I'll begin
After we had alighted at the Inn,
Then I'll report our journey, stage by stage,
All the remainder of our pilgrimage.
But first I beg of you, in courtesy, 745
Not to condemn me as unmannerly
If I speak plainly and with no concealings
And give account of all their words and dealings,
Using their very phrases as they fell.
For certainly, as you all know so well, 750
He who repeats a tale after a man
Is bound to say, as nearly as he can,
Each single word, if he remembers it,
However rudely spoken or unfit,
Or else the tale he tells will be untrue, 755
The things pretended and the phrases new.
He may not flinch although it were his brother,
He may as well say one word as another.
And Christ Himself spoke broad in Holy Writ,
Yet there is no scurrility in it, 760
And Plato says, for those with power to read,
"The word should be as cousin to the deed."

Offertory: a hymn sung during the offering in a church service
alighted: stepped down from one's horse
spoke broad in Holy Writ: spoke plainly about the Bible
scurrility: obscenity
Plato: ancient Greek philosopher; the teacher of Aristotle

Further I beg you to forgive it me
If I neglect the order and degree
And what is due to rank in what I've planned.   765
I'm short of wit as you will understand.
      Our *Host* gave us great welcome; everyone
Was given a place and supper was begun.
He served the finest victuals you could think,
The wine was strong and we were glad to drink.   770
A very striking man our Host withal,
And fit to be a marshal in a hall.
His eyes were bright, his girth a little wide;
There is no finer burgess in Cheapside.
Bold in his speech, yet wise and full of tact,   775
There was no manly attribute he lacked,
What's more he was a merry-hearted man.
After our meal he jokingly began
To talk of sport, and, among other things
After we'd settled up our reckonings,   780
He said as follows: "Truly, gentlemen,
You're very welcome and I can't think when
—Upon my word I'm telling you no lie—
I've seen a gathering here that looked so spry,
No, not this year, as in this tavern now.   785
I'd think you up some fun if I knew how.
And, as it happens, a thought has just occurred
To please you, costing nothing, on my word.
You're off to Canterbury—well, God speed!
Blessed St. Thomas answer to your need!   790
And I don't doubt, before the journey's done
You mean to while the time in tales and fun.
Indeed, there's little pleasure for your bones
Riding along and all as dumb as stones.
So let me then propose for your enjoyment,   795
Just as I said, a suitable employment.
And if my notion suits and you agree
And promise to submit yourselves to me

Cheapside: an area of markets in London

Playing your parts exactly as I say
Tomorrow as you ride along the way,   800
Then by my father's soul (and he is dead)
If you don't like it you can have my head!
Hold up your hands, and not another word."
    Well, our opinion was not long deferred,
It seemed not worth a serious debate;   805
We all agreed to it at any rate
And bade him issue what commands he would.
"My lords," he said, "now listen for your good,
And please don't treat my notion with disdain.
This is the point. I'll make it short and plain.   810
Each one of you shall help to make things slip
By telling two stories on the outward trip
To Canterbury, that's what I intend,
And, on the homeward way to journey's end
Another two, tales from the days of old;   815
And then the man whose story is best told,
That is to say who gives the fullest measure
Of good morality and general pleasure,
He shall be given a supper, paid by all,
Here in this tavern, in this very hall,   820
When we come back again from Canterbury.
And in the hope to keep you bright and merry
I'll go along with you myself and ride
All at my own expense and serve as guide.
I'll be the judge, and those who won't obey   825
Shall pay for what we spend upon the way.
Now if you all agree to what you've heard
Tell me at once without another word,
And I will make arrangements early for it."
    Of course we all agreed, in fact we swore it   830
Delightedly, and made entreaty too
That he should act as he proposed to do,
Become our Governor in short, and be
Judge of our tales and general referee,
And set the supper at a certain price.   835
We promised to be ruled by his advice

46

Come high, come low; unanimously thus
We set him up in judgment over us.
More wine was fetched, the business being done;
We drank it off and up went everyone   840
To bed without a moment of delay.
    Early next morning at the spring of day
Up rose our Host and roused us like a cock,
Gathering us together in a flock,
And off we rode at slightly faster pace   845
Than walking to St. Thomas' watering-place;
And there our Host drew up, began to ease
His horse, and said, "Now, listen if you please,
My lords! Remember what you promised me.
If evensong and matins will agree   850
Let's see who shall be first to tell a tale.
And as I hope to drink good wine and ale
I'll be your judge. The rebel who disobeys,
However much the journey costs, he pays.
Now draw for cut and then we can depart;   855
The man who draws the shortest cut shall start."

---

evensong and matins: church songs sung in evening and morning
    services, respectively
cut: a straw

from THE WIFE OF BATH'S TALE

Geoffrey Chaucer, translated by Nevill Coghill

The Wife of Bath, a bawdy and vivacious character, is one of the pilgrims the narrator of the Prologue describes. Readers learn that she has "had five husbands, all at the church door." In the complete Prologue to her own humorous tale (which has been greatly abbreviated below), the quick-witted Wife of Bath recounts her five marriages, describes her husbands' flaws, explains the problems she faced with each of them, and admits to the mistakes that she made in her relationships. She establishes herself as an authority on marriage, and, using humor and allusions to ancient and medieval texts, she explores the theme of what men and women should do in a marriage. Her tale, like many others in The Canterbury Tales, *is a vivid retelling of an older legend. It focuses on a knight who must go on a quest to discover what women truly want.*

THE PROLOGUE

The Pardoner started up, and thereupon
"Madam," he said, "by God and by St. John,
That's noble preaching no one could surpass!
I was about to take a wife; alas!
Am I to buy it on my flesh so dear?   5
There'll be no marrying for me this year!"
　　"You wait," she said, "my story's not begun.
You'll taste another brew before I've done;
You'll find it doesn't taste as good as ale;
And when I've finished telling you my tale   10
Of tribulation in the married life
In which I've been an expert as a wife,
That is to say, myself have been the whip.

---

tribulation: ordeal; suffering
whip: the party causing pain in a relationship

48

So please yourself whether you want to sip
At that same cask of marriage I shall broach.   15
Be cautious before making the approach,
For I'll give instances, and more than ten.
And those who won't be warned by other men,
By other men shall suffer their correction,
So Ptolemy has said, in this connection.   20
You read his *Almagest*; you'll find it there."

    "Madam, I put it to you as a prayer,"
The Pardoner said, "go on as you began!
Tell us your tale, spare not for any man.
Instruct us younger men in your technique."   25
"Gladly," she said, "if you will let me speak,
But still I hope the company won't reprove me
Though I should speak as fantasy may move me,
And please don't be offended at my views;
They're really only offered to amuse."...   30

THE TALE

When good King Arthur ruled in ancient days
(A king that every Briton loves to praise)
This was a land brim-full of fairy folk.
The Elf-Queen and her courtiers joined and broke
Their elfin dance on many a green mead,   35
Or so was the opinion once, I read,
Hundreds of years ago, in days of yore.

---

cask: a large barrel, often filled with wine
broach: to tap; to allow to begin flowing
Ptolemy: an ancient mathematician, astronomer, and geographer
    who lived in Egypt
Almagest: a book, also known as *Mathematical Composition*, written
    by Ptolemy that asserted that the earth is the center of the
    universe, a belief held by medieval people
reprove: criticize; reprimand
King Arthur: legendary king of England
Briton: a resident of the island of Great Britain
courtiers: attendants
mead: meadow

But no one now sees fairies any more.
For now the saintly charity and prayer
Of holy friars seem to have purged the air;   40
They search the countryside through field and
    stream
As thick as motes that speckle a sun-beam,
Blessing the halls, the chambers, kitchens, bowers,
Cities and boroughs, castles, courts and towers,
Thorpes, barns and stables, outhouses and dairies,   45
And that's the reason why there are no fairies.
Wherever there was wont to walk an elf
To-day there walks the holy friar himself
As evening falls or when the daylight springs,
Saying his matins and his holy things,   50
Walking his limit round from town to town.
Women can now go safely up and down
By every bush or under every tree;
There is no other incubus but he,
So there is really no one else to hurt you   55
And he will do no more than take your virtue.
    Now it so happened, I began to say,
Long, long ago in good King Arthur's day,
There was a knight who was a lusty liver.
One day as he came riding from the river   60
He saw a maiden walking all forlorn
Ahead of him, alone as she was born.
And of that maiden, spite of all she said,
By very force he took her maidenhead.
    This act of violence made such a stir,   65
So much petitioning to the king for her,
That he condemned the knight to lose his head

---

purged: cleansed
motes: tiny particles of dust
bowers: bedrooms
thorpes: small villages
incubus: an evil spirit that attacks sleeping women
virtue: morality; in this case it suggests chastity or purity
maidenhead: virginity

By course of law. He was as good as dead
(It seems that then the statutes took that view)
But that the queen, and other ladies too,   70
Implored the king to exercise his grace
So ceaselessly, he gave the queen the case
And granted her his life, and she could choose
Whether to show him mercy or refuse.

  The queen returned him thanks with all her might, 75
And then she sent a summons to the knight
At her convenience, and expressed her will:
"You stand, for such is the position still,
In no way certain of your life," said she,
"Yet you shall live if you can answer me: 80
What is the thing that women most desire?
Beware the axe and say as I require.

  "If you can't answer on the moment, though,
I will concede you this: You are to go
A twelvemonth and a day to seek and learn   85
Sufficient answer, then you shall return.
I shall take gages from you to extort
Surrender of your body to the court."

  Sad was the knight and sorrowfully sighed,
But there! All other choices were denied,   90
And in the end he chose to go away
And to return after a year and day
Armed with such answer as there might be sent
To him by God. He took his leave and went.

  He knocked at every house, searched every place, 95
Yes, anywhere that offered hope of grace.
What could it be that women wanted most?
But all the same he never touched a coast,
Country, or town in which there seemed to be
Any two people willing to agree.   100

---

implored: begged
twelvemonth: a year
take gages from you: requires pledges of you
extort: extract by force

Some said that women wanted wealth and
  treasure,
"Honor," said some, some "Jollity and pleasure,"
Some "Gorgeous clothes" and others "Fun in bed,"
"To be oft widowed and remarried," said
Others again, and some that what most mattered   105
Was that we should be cosseted and flattered.
That's very near the truth, it seems to me;
A man can win us best with flattery.
To dance attendance on us, make a fuss,
Ensnares us all, the best and worst of us.   110
    Some say the things we most desire are these:
Freedom to do exactly as we please,
With no one to reprove our faults and lies,
Rather to have one call us good and wise.
Truly there's not a woman in ten score   115
Who has a fault, and someone rubs the sore,
But she will kick if what he says is true;
You try it out and you will find so too.
However vicious we may be within
We like to be thought wise and void of sin.   120
Others assert we women find it sweet
When we are thought dependable, discreet
And secret, firm of purpose and controlled,
Never betraying things that we are told.
But that's not worth the handle of a rake;   125
Women conceal a thing? For Heaven's sake!
Remember Midas? Will you hear the tale?
    Among some other little things, now stale,

---

jollity: good times
cosseted: pleased; pampered
ten score: two hundred (a score is 20)
Midas: a legendary king in Greek mythology

Ovid relates that under his long hair
The unhappy Midas grew a splendid pair   130
Of ass's ears; as subtly as he might,
He kept his foul deformity from sight;
Save for his wife, there was not one that knew.
He loved her best, and trusted in her too.
He begged her not to tell a living creature   135
That he possessed so horrible a feature.
And she—she swore, were all the world to win,
She would not do such villainy and sin
As saddle her husband with so foul a name;
Besides to speak would be to share the shame.   140
Nevertheless she thought she would have died
Keeping this secret bottled up inside;
It seemed to swell her heart and she, no doubt,
Thought it was on the point of bursting out.
        Fearing to speak of it to woman or man,   145
Down to a reedy marsh she quickly ran
And reached the sedge. Her heart was all on fire
And, as a bittern bumbles in the mire,
She whispered to the water, near the ground,
"Betray me not, O water, with thy sound!   150
To thee alone I tell it: It appears
My husband has a pair of ass's ears!
Ah! My heart's well again, the secret's out!
I could no longer keep it, not a doubt."
And so you see, although we may hold fast   155

Ovid: an ancient Roman writer known best for his love poetry and
    the myths he recorded; in his Midas story, it is King Midas's
    barber, not his wife, who betrays the secret of the king's ears;
    reeds grow in the hole into which the barber has spoken and
    the reeds whisper the secret whenever the wind rustles through
    them
subtly: carefully, so as not to draw attention to something
saddle: burden
sedge: small, grassy plants that grow on the edges of swamps and
    marshlands
bittern: a type of heron that lives in swamps and is known for its
    loud call

A little while, it must come out at last,
We can't keep secrets; as for Midas, well,
Read Ovid for his story; he will tell.

    This knight that I am telling you about
Perceived at last he never would find out   160
What it could be that women loved the best.
Faint was the soul within his sorrowful breast,
As home he went, he dared no longer stay;
His year was up and now it was the day.

    As he rode home in a dejected mood   165
Suddenly, at the margin of a wood,
He saw a dance upon the leafy floor
Of four and twenty ladies, nay, and more.
Eagerly he approached, in hope to learn
Some words of wisdom ere he should return;   170
But lo! Before he came to where they were,
Dancers and dance all vanished into air!
There wasn't a living creature to be seen
Save one old woman crouched upon the green.
A fouler-looking creature I suppose   175
Could scarcely be imagined. She arose
And said, "Sir knight, there's no way on from here.
Tell me what you are looking for, my dear,
For peradventure that were best for you;
We old, old women know a thing or two."   180

    "Dear Mother," said the knight, "alack the day!
I am as good as dead if I can't say
What thing it is that women most desire;
If you could tell me I would pay your hire."
"Give me your hand," she said, "and swear to do   185
Whatever I shall next require of you
—If so to do should lie within your might—
And you shall know the answer before night."
"Upon my honor," he answered, "I agree."

---

margin: edge
peradventure: possibly; perhaps
alack: an expression of grief or sorrow

"Then," said the crone, "I dare to guarantee   190
Your life is safe; I shall make good my claim.
Upon my life the queen will say the same.
Show me the very proudest of them all
In costly coverchief or jeweled caul
That dare say no to what I have to teach.   195
Let us go forward without further speech."
And then she crooned her gospel in his ear
And told him to be glad and not to fear.

  They came to court. This knight, in full array,
Stood forth and said, "O Queen, I've kept my day   200
And kept my word and have my answer ready."

  There sat the noble matrons and the heady
Young girls, and widows too, that have the grace
Of wisdom, all assembled in that place,
And there the queen herself was throned to hear   205
And judge his answer. Then the knight drew near
And silence was commanded through the hall.

  The queen gave order he should tell them all
What thing it was that women wanted most.
He stood not silent like a beast or post,   210
But gave his answer with the ringing word
Of a man's voice and the assembly heard:

  "My liege and lady, in general," said he,
"A woman wants the self-same sovereignty
Over her husband as over her lover,   215
And master him; he must not be above her.
That is your greatest wish, whether you kill
Or spare me; please yourself. I wait your will."

  In all the court not one that shook her head
Or contradicted what the knight had said;   220

---

crone: hag; ugly woman
coverchief: a scarf or covering worn on the head
caul: a headdress that covers a woman's hair
crooned: sang
in full array: in full uniform; in fine clothing
liege: a person with power
sovereignty: power

Maid, wife, and widow cried, "He's saved his life!"
 And on the word up started the old wife,
The one the knight saw sitting on the green,
And cried, "Your mercy, sovereign lady queen!
Before the court disperses, do me right!   225
'Twas I who taught this answer to the knight,
For which he swore, and pledged his honor to it,
That the first thing I asked of him he'd do it,
So far as it should lie within his might.
Before this court I ask you then, sir knight,   230
To keep your word and take me for your wife;
For well you know that I have saved your life.
If this be false, deny it on your sword!"
 "Alas!" he said, "Old lady, by the Lord
I know indeed that such was my behest,   235
But for God's love think of a new request,
Take all my goods, but leave my body free."
"A curse on us," she said, "if I agree!
I may be foul, I may be poor and old,
Yet will not choose to be, for all the gold   240
That's bedded in the earth or lies above,
Less than your wife, nay, than your very love!"
 "My love?" said he. "By heaven, my damnation!
Alas that any of my race and station
Should ever make so foul a misalliance!"   245
Yet in the end his pleading and defiance
All went for nothing, he was forced to wed.
He takes his ancient wife and goes to bed.
 Now peradventure some may well suspect
A lack of care in me since I neglect   250
To tell of the rejoicings and display
Made at the feast upon their wedding-day.
I have but a short answer to let fall;
I say there was no joy or feast at all,

---

disperses: recesses; lets out
behest: command
damnation: curse
misalliance: an unsuitable marriage

Nothing but heaviness of heart and sorrow.   255
He married her in private on the morrow
And all day long stayed hidden like an owl,
It was such torture that his wife looked foul.
    Great was the anguish churning in his head
When he and she were piloted to bed;   260
He wallowed back and forth in desperate style.
His ancient wife lay smiling all the while;
At last she said "Bless us! Is this, my dear,
How knights and wives get on together here?
Are these the laws of good King Arthur's house?   265
Are knights of his all so contemptuous?
I am your own beloved and your wife,
And I am she, indeed, that saved your life;
And certainly I never did you wrong.
Then why, this first of nights, so sad a song?   270
You're carrying on as if you were half-witted
Say, for God's love, what sin have I committed?
I'll put things right if you will tell me how."
    "Put right?" he cried. "That never can be now!
Nothing can ever be put right again!   275
You're old, and so abominably plain,
So poor to start with, so low-bred to follow;
It's little wonder if I twist and wallow!
God, that my heart would burst within my breast!"
    "Is that," said she, "the cause of your unrest?"   280
    "Yes, certainly," he said, "and can you wonder?"
    "I could set right what you suppose a blunder,
That's if I cared to, in a day or two,
If I were shown more courtesy by you.
Just now," she said, "you spoke of gentle birth,   285
Such as descends from ancient wealth and worth.

---

on the morrow: the next day
churning: turning over and over
wallowed: rolled around
contemptuous: disapproving
low-bred: of an undistinguished and non-noble background
gentle birth: nobility; being born into the aristocracy

If that's the claim you make for gentlemen
Such arrogance is hardly worth a hen.
Whoever loves to work for virtuous ends,
Public and private, and who most intends   290
To do what deeds of gentleness he can,
Take him to be the greatest gentleman.
Christ wills we take our gentleness from Him,
Not from a wealth of ancestry long dim,
Though they bequeath their whole establishment   295
By which we claim to be of high descent.
Our fathers cannot make us a bequest
Of all those virtues that became them best
And earned for them the name of gentlemen,
But bade us follow them as best we can.   300
    "Thus the wise poet of the Florentines,
Dante by name, has written in these lines,
For such is the opinion Dante launches:
'Seldom arises by these slender branches
Prowess of men, for it is God, no less,   305
Wills us to claim of Him our gentleness.'
For of our parents nothing can we claim
Save temporal things, and these may hurt and maim.
    "But everyone knows this as well as I;
For if gentility were implanted by   310
The natural course of lineage down the line,
Public or private, could it cease to shine
In doing the fair work of gentle deed?
No vice or villainy could then bear seed.
    "Take fire and carry it to the darkest house   315

---

arrogance: extreme pride
virtuous: morally upright
long dim: long dead
bequeath: pass on
Dante: Italian poet who wrote *The Divine Comedy*
prowess: competence
temporal: temporary; not permanent
maim: mutilate or disfigure
gentility: manners; propriety
vice: faults

Between this kingdom and the Caucasus,
And shut the doors on it and leave it there,
It will burn on, and it will burn as fair
As if ten thousand men were there to see,
For fire will keep its nature and degree,   320
I can assure you, sir, until it dies.
    "But gentleness, as you will recognize,
Is not annexed in nature to possessions.
Men fail in living up to their professions;
But fire never ceases to be fire.   325
God knows you'll often find, if you inquire,
Some lording full of villainy and shame.
If you would be esteemed for the mere name
Of having been by birth a gentleman
And stemming from some virtuous, noble clan,   330
And do not live yourself by gentle deed
Or take your father's noble code and creed,
You are no gentleman, though duke or earl.
Vice and bad manners are what make a churl.
    "Gentility is only the renown   335
For bounty that your fathers handed down,
Quite foreign to your person, not your own;
Gentility must come from God alone.
That we are gentle comes to us by grace
And by no means is it bequeathed with place.   340
    "Reflect how noble (says Valerius)
Was Tullius surnamed Hostilius,
Who rose from poverty to nobleness.

Caucasus: a mountain range containing Europe's highest mountain,
    located in modern-day Russia
annexed: connected; linked
lording: a lord's son
churl: a foul-tempered person
renown: reputation
Valerius: Valerius Maximus, a first-century Roman author who
    wrote about the treatment of women in marriage
Tullius surnamed Hostilius: the third king of ancient Rome in the
    seventh century B.C.

And read Boethius, Seneca no less,
Thus they express themselves and are agreed: 345
'Gentle is he that does a gentle deed.'
And therefore, my dear husband, I conclude
That even if my ancestors were rude,
Yet God on high—and so I hope He will—
Can grant me grace to live in virtue still,   350
A gentlewoman only when beginning
To live in virtue and to shrink from sinning.
　　"As for my poverty which you reprove,
Almighty God Himself in whom we move,
Believe, and have our being, chose a life   355
Of poverty, and every man or wife
Nay, every child can see our Heavenly King
Would never stoop to choose a shameful thing.
No shame in poverty if the heart is gay,
As Seneca and all the learned say.   360
He who accepts his poverty unhurt
I'd say is rich although he lacked a shirt.
But truly poor are they who whine and fret
And covet what they cannot hope to get.
And he that, having nothing, covets not,   365
Is rich, though you may think he is a sot.
　　"True poverty can find a song to sing.
Juvenal says a pleasant little thing:
'The poor can dance and sing in the relief
Of having nothing that will tempt a thief.'   370
Though it be hateful, poverty is good,
A great incentive to a livelihood,
And a great help to our capacity
For wisdom, if accepted patiently.

Boethius: an important Roman writer and philosopher of the fifth
　　and sixth centuries
Seneca: an ancient Roman author and orator who was highly
　　regarded in the Middle Ages
covet: crave, especially something that one does not have
sot: a fool
Juvenal: a first-century Roman satirist

Poverty is, though wanting in estate,   375
A kind of wealth that none calumniate.
Poverty often, when the heart is lowly,
Brings one to God and teaches what is holy,
Gives knowledge of oneself and even lends
A glass by which to see one's truest friends.   380
And since it's no offense, let me be plain;
Do not rebuke my poverty again.

    "Lastly you taxed me, sir, with being old.
Yet even if you never had been told
By ancient books, you gentlemen engage   385
Yourselves in honor to respect old age.
To call an old man 'father' shows good breeding,
And this could be supported from my reading.

    "You say I'm old and fouler than a fen.
You need not fear to be a cuckold, then.   390
Filth and old age, I'm sure you will agree,
Are powerful wardens over chastity.
Nevertheless, well knowing your delights,
I shall fulfill your worldly appetites.

    "You have two choices; which one will you try?   395
To have me old and ugly till I die,
But still a loyal, true, and humble wife
That never will displease you all her life,
Or would you rather I were young and pretty
And chance your arm what happens in a city   400
Where friends will visit you because of me,
Yes, and in other places too, maybe.
Which would you have? The choice is all your own."

    The knight thought long, and with a piteous groan
At last he said, with all the care in life,   405
"My lady and my love, my dearest wife,
I leave the matter to your wise decision.

---

calumniate: make false statements or accusations about
taxed: accused; burdened
fen: swamp
cuckold: a man whose wife is unfaithful to him
wardens: guards

You make the choice yourself, for the provision
Of what may be agreeable and rich
In honor to us both, I don't care which;   410
Whatever pleases you suffices me."
    "And have I won the mastery?" said she,
"Since I'm to choose and rule as I think fit?"
"Certainly, wife," he answered her, "that's it."
"Kiss me," she cried. "No quarrels! On my oath   415
And word of honor, you shall find me both,
That is, both fair and faithful as a wife;
May I go howling mad and take my life
Unless I prove to be as good and true
As ever wife was since the world was new!   420
And if to-morrow when the sun's above
I seem less fair than any lady-love,
Than any queen or empress east or west,
Do with my life and death as you think best.
Cast up the curtain, husband. Look at me!"   425
    And when indeed the knight had looked to see,
Lo, she was young and lovely, rich in charms.
In ecstasy he caught her in his arms,
His heart went bathing in a bath of blisses
And melted in a hundred thousand kisses,   430
And she responded in the fullest measure
With all that could delight or give him pleasure.
    So they lived ever after to the end
In perfect bliss; and may Christ Jesus send
Us husbands meek and young and fresh in bed,   435
And grace to overbid them when we wed.
And—Jesu hear my prayer!—cut short the lives
Of those who won't be governed by their wives;
And all old, angry niggards of their pence,
God send them soon a very pestilence!   440

---

suffices me: is sufficient for me
niggards: misers; extremely stingy people
pestilence: plague; disease

LOVE
SONNETS

Petrarchan Sonnets

Francesco Petrarcha

Francesco Petrarcha (1304–1374), known as Petrarch, was an Italian poet of the early Renaissance. He is the father of the Petrarchan sonnet, a poetic form that influenced generations of European writers. Petrarch's fourteenth-century sonnets were addressed to an idealized beloved named Laura.

Sonnet 18

Translated by Noti

Ashamed sometimes thy beauties should remain
As yet unsung, sweet lady, in my rhyme;
When first I saw thee I recall the time.
Pleasing as none shall ever please again.
But no fit polish can my verse attain,   5
Not mine is strength to try the task sublime:
My genius, measuring its power to climb,
From such attempt doth prudently refrain.
Full oft I oped my lips to chant thy name;
Then in mid-utterance the lay was lost: 10
But say what muse can dare so bold a flight?
Full oft I strove in measure to indite;
But ah, the pen, the hand, the vein I boast,
At once were vanquish'd by the mighty theme!

---

prudently: cautiously or carefully
oft: often
oped: opened
lay: arrangement
in measure: in poetry
indite: compose or write
vanquish'd: defeated

SONNET 28

Anonymous Translator

Alone, and lost in thought, the desert glade
Measuring I roam with ling'ring steps and slow;
And still a watchful glance around me throw,
Anxious to shun the print of human tread:
No other means I find, no surer aid   5
From the world's prying eye to hide my woe:
So well my wild disorder'd gestures show,
And lovelorn looks, the fire within me bred,
That well I deem each mountain, wood and plain,
And river knows, what I from man conceal,   10
What dreary hues my life's fond prospects dim.
Yet whate'er wild or savage paths I've ta'en,
Where'er I wander, love attends me still,
Soft whisp'ring to my soul, and I to him.

---

glade: a clearing
shun: reject; turn away from
lovelorn: unloved; lovesick
prospects: hopes

SHAKESPEAREAN SONNETS

William Shakespeare

William Shakespeare (1564–1616) wrote more than 150 sonnets, most of which were first published in 1609, although their dates of composition are unknown. Shakespearean, or English, sonnets differ from Petrarchan sonnets in their form and rhyme scheme. The speaker in Shakespeare's sonnets frequently refers to interactions with various people including a handsome young man, a dark lady, and a rival poet.

SONNET 18

Shall I compare thee to a summer's day?
Thou art more lovely and more temperate:
Rough winds do shake the darling buds of May,
And summer's lease hath all too short a date;
Sometime too hot the eye of heaven shines,   5
And often is his gold complexion dimmed;
And every fair from fair sometime declines,
By chance or nature's changing course untrimmed.
But thy eternal summer shall not fade,
Nor lose possession of that fair thou ow'st;   10
Nor shall death brag thou wander'st in his shade,
When in eternal lines to time thou grow'st:
    So long as men can breathe or eyes can see,
    So long lives this, and this gives life to thee.

---

temperate: mild
lease: term of existence
untrimmed: stripped of adornments
ow'st: own

Sonnet 29

When, in disgrace with Fortune and men's eyes,
I all alone beweep my outcast state,
And trouble deaf heaven with my bootless cries,
And look upon myself and curse my fate,
Wishing me like to one more rich in hope,   5
Featured like him, like him with friends possessed,
Desiring this man's art and that man's scope,
With what I most enjoy contented least;
Yet in these thoughts myself almost despising,
Haply I think on thee, and then my state   10
(Like to the lark at break of day arising
From sullen earth) sings hymns at heaven's gate;
 For thy sweet love remembered such wealth brings
 That then I scorn to change my state with kings.

Fortune: fate; destiny
beweep: to weep over
bootless: useless
art: skill
scope: range of knowledge
haply: by chance

Sonnet 30

When to the sessions of sweet silent thought
I summon up remembrance of things past,
I sigh the lack of many a thing I sought,
And with old woes new wail my dear time's waste:
Then can I drown an eye (unused to flow)   5
For precious friends hid in death's dateless night,
And weep afresh love's long since canceled woe,
And moan th' expense of many a vanished sight:
Then can I grieve at grievances foregone,
And heavily from woe to woe tell o'er   10
The sad account of fore-bemoanèd moan,
Which I new pay as if not paid before.
    But if the while I think on thee, dear friend,
    All losses are restored and sorrows end.

Sonnet 73

That time of year thou mayst in me behold
When yellow leaves, or none, or few, do hang
Upon those boughs which shake against the cold,
Bare ruined choirs, where late the sweet birds sang.
In me thou seest the twilight of such day   5
As after sunset fadeth in the west;
Which by and by black night doth take away,
Death's second self that seals up all in rest.
In me thou seest the glowing of such fire
That on the ashes of his youth doth lie,   10
As the deathbed whereon it must expire,
Consumed with that which it was nourished by.
  This thou perceiv'st, which makes thy love more strong,
  To love that well, which thou must leave ere long.

---

choirs: part of the church where divine service was sung
ere: before

Sonnet 78

So oft have I invok'd thee for my Muse
And found such fair assistance in my verse
As every alien pen hath got my use
And under thee their poesy disperse.
Thine eyes, that taught the dumb on high to sing   5
And heavy ignorance aloft to fly,
Have added feathers to the learned's wing
And given grace a double majesty.
Yet be most proud of that which I compile,
Whose influence is thine, and born of thee: 10
In others' works thou dost but mend the style,
And arts with thy sweet graces graced be;
    But thou art all my art, and dost advance
    As high as learning my rude ignorance.

---

invok'd: called upon; summoned
Muse: a source of inspiration, alluding to the Muses of Greek
    mythology—the nine daughters of Zeus who were believed to
    inspire and protect artists
poesy: poetry

Sonnet 106

When in the chronicle of wasted time
I see descriptions of the fairest wights,
And beauty making beautiful old rhyme
In praise of ladies dead and lovely knights,
Then, in the blazon of sweet beauty's best,   5
Of hand, of foot, of lip, of eye, of brow,
I see their antique pen would have expressed
Even such a beauty as you master now.
So all their praises are but prophecies
Of this our time, all you prefiguring;   10
And, for they looked but with divining eyes,
They had not skill enough your worth to sing:
    For we, which now behold these present days,
    Have eyes to wonder, but lack tongues to praise.

---

wights: people; human beings
blazon: catalog
divining: predicting; prophetic

Sonnet 116

Let me not to the marriage of true minds
Admit impediments; love is not love
Which alters when it alteration finds,
Or bends with the remover to remove:
O, no, it is an ever-fixèd mark,   5
That looks on tempests and is never shaken;
It is the star to every wand'ring bark,
Whose worth's unknown, although his highth be taken.
Love's not Time's fool, though rosy lips and cheeks
Within his bending sickle's compass come;   10
Love alters not with his brief hours and weeks,
But bears it out even to the edge of doom.
    If this be error and upon me proved,
    I never writ, nor no man ever loved.

---

impediments: hindrances
sickle: a tool with a curved blade, used to harvest grains
writ: wrote

Sonnet 130

My mistress' eyes are nothing like the sun;
Coral is far more red than her lips' red;
If snow be white, why then her breasts are dun;
If hairs be wires, black wires grow on her head.
I have seen roses damasked, red and white,   5
But no such roses see I in her cheeks;
And in some perfumes is there more delight
Than in the breath that from my mistress reeks.
I love to hear her speak, yet well I know
That music hath a far more pleasing sound;   10
I grant I never saw a goddess go;
My mistress, when she walks, treads on the ground.
    And yet, by heaven, I think my love as rare
    As any she belied with false compare.

---

dun: a dull gray-brown color
damasked: mixed
reeks: is exhaled
belied: misrepresented

from SONNETS FROM THE PORTUGUESE

Elizabeth Barrett Browning

These sonnets, written by Elizabeth Barrett Browning (1806–1861), are from Sonnets from the Portuguese. *Published in 1850, the collection is a record of the courtship between Elizabeth and her future husband and fellow poet Robert Browning.*

SONNET 10

Yet, love, mere love, is beautiful indeed
And worthy of acceptation. Fire is bright,
Let temple burn, or flax; an equal light
Leaps in the flame from cedar-plank or weed:
And love is fire. And when I say at need   5
I love thee...mark!...*I love thee!*—in thy sight
I stand transfigured, glorified aright,
With conscience of the new rays that proceed
Out of my face toward thine. There's nothing low
In love, when love the lowest: meanest creatures   10
Who love God, God accepts while loving so.
And what I *feel*, across the inferior features
Of what I *am*, doth flash itself, and show
How that great work of Love enhances Nature's.

---

flax: a plant whose fibers can be made into thread and woven into
    fabric
transfigured: elevated or idealized

Sonnet 11

And therefore if to love can be desert,
I am not all unworthy. Cheeks as pale
As these you see, and trembling knees that fail
To bear the burden of a heavy heart,—
This weary minstrel-life that once was girt   5
To climb Aornus, and can scarce avail
To pipe now 'gainst the valley nightingale
A melancholy music,—why advert
To these things? O Belovèd, it is plain
I am not of thy worth nor for thy place!   10
And yet, because I love thee, I obtain
From that same love this vindicating grace,
To live on still in love, and yet in vain,—
To bless thee, yet renounce thee to thy face.

---

minstrel-life: a life spent moving from place to place; an unsettled
    life
girt: prepared; readied
Aornus: a legendarily tall rock fortress in India that was conquered
    by Alexander the Great
scarce avail: barely attempt
pipe: sing
advert: refer

Sonnet 12

Indeed this very love which is my boast,
And which, when rising up from breast to brow,
Doth crown me with a ruby large enow
To draw men's eyes and prove the inner cost,—
This love even, all my worth, to the uttermost,   5
I should not love withal, unless that thou
Hadst set me an example, shown me how,
When first thine earnest eyes with mine were crossed,
And love called love. And thus, I cannot speak
Of love even, as a good thing of my own: 10
Thy soul hath snatched up mine all faint and weak,
And placed it by thee on a golden throne,—
And that I love (O soul, we must be meek!)
Is by thee only, whom I love alone.

Sonnet 13

And wilt thou have me fashion into speech
The love I bear thee, finding words enough,
And hold the torch out, while the winds are rough,
Between our faces, to cast light on each?—
I drop it at thy feet. I cannot teach   5
My hand to hold my spirit so far off
From myself—me—that I should bring thee proof
In words, of love hid in me out of reach.
Nay, let the silence of my womanhood
Commend my woman-love to thy belief,—   10
Seeing that I stand unwon, however wooed,
And rend the garment of my life, in brief,
By a most dauntless, voiceless fortitude,
Lest one touch of this heart convey its grief.

---

enow: enough
rend: tear
dauntless: fearless; determined

Sonnet 14

If thou must love me, let it be for nought
Except for love's sake only. Do not say
"I love her for her smile—her look—her way
Of speaking gently,—for a trick of thought
That falls in well with mine, and certes brought   5
A sense of pleasant ease on such a day"—
For these things in themselves, Belovèd, may
Be changed, or change for thee,—and love, so wrought,
May be unwrought so. Neither love me for
Thine own dear pity's wiping my cheeks dry,—   10
A creature might forget to weep, who bore
Thy comfort long, and lose thy love thereby!
But love me for love's sake, that evermore
Thou mayst love on, through love's eternity.

Sonnet 43

How do I love thee? Let me count the ways.
I love thee to the depth and breadth and height
My soul can reach, when feeling out of sight
For the ends of Being and ideal Grace.
I love thee to the level of everyday's   5
Most quiet need, by sun and candle-light.
I love thee freely, as men strive for Right;
I love thee purely, as they turn from Praise.
I love thee with a passion put to use
In my old griefs, and with my childhood's faith.   10
I love thee with a love I seemed to lose
With my lost saints,—I love thee with the breath,
Smiles, tears, of all my life!—and, if God choose,
I shall but love thee better after death.

---

nought: nothing
certes: certain
wrought: shaped; created

Two Sonnets

Pablo Neruda, translated by Stephen Tapscott

Pablo Neruda (1904–1973) was a twentieth-century Chilean poet and diplomat. He won the Nobel Prize in Literature in 1971. These two sonnets were first published in Cien Sonetos de Amor, *known in English as* 100 Love Sonnets. *The works in this volume were inspired by and dedicated to the poet's wife, Matilde Urrutia.*

Sonnet 17

I do not love you as if you were salt-rose, or topaz,
or the arrow of carnations the fire shoots off.
I love you as certain dark things are to be loved,
in secret, between the shadow and the soul.

I love you as the plant that never blooms   5
but carries in itself the light of hidden flowers;
thanks to your love a certain solid fragrance,
risen from the earth, lives darkly in my body.

I love you without knowing how, or when, or
    from where.
I love you straightforwardly, without   10
    complexities or pride;
so I love you because I know no other way

than this: where *I* does not exist, nor *you*,
so close that your hand on my chest is my hand,
so close that your eyes close as I fall asleep.

---

salt-rose: rock salt formed from ancient sea salt deposits that were
    then covered by volcanic lava, thus giving it a ruby coloring
topaz: a gemstone

Soneto 17

No te amo como si fueras rosa de sal, topacio
o flecha de claveles que propagan el fuego:
te amo como se aman ciertas cosas oscuras,
secretamente, entre la sombra y el alma.

Te amo como la planta que no florece y lleva   5
dentro de sí, escondida, la luz de aquellas flores,
y gracias a tu amor vive oscuro en mi cuerpo
el apretado aroma que ascendió de la tierra.

Te amo sin saber cómo, ni cuándo, ni de dónde,
te amo directamente sin problemas ni orgullo: 10
así te amo porque no sé amar de otra manera,

sino así de este modo en que no soy ni eres,
tan cerca que tu mano sobre mi pecho es mía,
tan cerca que se cierran tus ojos con mi sueño.

Sonnet 79

By night, Love, tie your heart to mine, and the two
together in their sleep will defeat the darkness
like a double drum in the forest, pounding
against the thick wall of wet leaves.

Night travel: black flame of sleep   5
that snips the threads of the earth's grapes,
punctual as a headlong train that would haul
shadows and cold rocks, endlessly.

Because of this, Love, tie me to a purer motion,
to the constancy that beats in your chest   10
with the wings of a swan underwater,

so that our sleep might answer all the sky's
starry questions with a single key,
with a single door the shadows had closed.

Soneto 79

De noche, amada, amarra tu corazón al mío
y que ellos en el sueño derroten las tinieblas
como un doble tambor combatiendo en el bosque
contra el espeso muro de las hojas mojadas.

Nocturna travesía, brasa negra del sueño   5
interceptando el hilo de las uvas terrestres
con la puntualidad de un tren descabellado
que sombra y piedras frías sin cesar arrastrara.

Por eso, amor, amárrame al movimiento puro,
a la tenacidad que en tu pecho golpea   10
con las alas de un cisne sumergido,

para que a las preguntas estrelladas del cielo
responda nuestro sueño con una sola llave,
con una sola puerta cerrada por la sombra.

Romantic
Poetry

from SONGS OF INNOCENCE
AND OF EXPERIENCE

William Blake

Both a poet and a visual artist, William Blake (1757–1827) published many of his poems with vivid engravings of his own design. In 1789, he published a collection of short poems, Songs of Innocence. *In 1794, he published* Songs of Innocence and of Experience, *which included the earlier poems in* Songs of Innocence *and added a new series of poems, the* Songs of Experience. *The two collections represent what Blake called "two contrary states of the human soul." The* Songs of Innocence *mostly present a childlike view of the world. Some of the* Songs of Experience *are closely related to poems from the earlier volume, but express a viewpoint informed by an awareness of suffering and evil.*

The following pages present a selection of companion poems from Songs of Innocence and of Experience:

SONGS OF INNOCENCE
The Chimney Sweeper [1]
The Divine Image
Infant Joy

SONGS OF EXPERIENCE
The Chimney Sweeper [2]
A Divine Image
Infant Sorrow

The Chimney Sweeper [1]

When my mother died I was very young,
And my father sold me while yet my tongue
Could scarcely cry weep weep weep weep.
So your chimneys I sweep & in soot I sleep.

There's little Tom Dacre, who cried when his head   5
That curl'd like a lamb's back, was shav'd, so I said,
"Hush, Tom! never mind it, for when your head's bare,
You know that the soot cannot spoil your white hair."

And so he was quiet, & that very night,
As Tom was a-sleeping he had such a sight,   10
That thousands of sweepers, Dick, Joe, Ned & Jack
Were all of them lock'd up in coffins of black;

And by came an Angel who had a bright key,
And he open'd the coffins & set them all free;
Then down a green plain leaping laughing they run, 15
And wash in a river and shine in the Sun.

Then naked & white, all their bags left behind,
They rise upon clouds, and sport in the wind.
And the Angel told Tom, if he'd be a good boy,
He'd have God for his father & never want joy.   20

And so Tom awoke and we rose in the dark
And got with our bags & our brushes to work.
Tho' the morning was cold, Tom was happy & warm,
So if all do their duty, they need not fear harm.

---

chimney sweeper: In Blake's time, young boys often did the
    dangerous and dirty task of cleaning fireplace chimneys. Many
    suffered respiratory disease and other ailments, including
    permanently blackened skin and legs that were bent from
    carrying heavy loads.
weep weep weep weep: A near-echo of the chimney sweeper's
    street cry, "Sweep, sweep, sweep...."

The Chimney Sweeper [2]

A little black thing among the snow:
Crying weep, weep, in notes of woe!
"Where are thy father & mother? say?"
"They are both gone up to the church to pray.

"Because I was happy upon the heath,   5
And smil'd among the winter's snow:
They clothed me in the clothes of death,
And taught me to sing the notes of woe.

"And because I am happy, & dance & sing,
They think they have done me no injury: 10
And are gone to praise God & his Priest & King
Who make up a heaven of our misery."

---

heath: a tract of land with few plants or trees

THE DIVINE IMAGE

To Mercy, Pity, Peace, and Love,
All pray in their distress,
And to these virtues of delight
Return their thankfulness.

For Mercy, Pity, Peace, and Love,   5
Is God, our father dear:
And Mercy, Pity, Peace, and Love,
Is Man, his child and care.

For Mercy has a human heart,
Pity, a human face,   10
And Love, the human form divine,
And Peace, the human dress.

Then every man of every clime,
That prays in his distress,
Prays to the human form divine,   15
Love, Mercy, Pity, Peace.

And all must love the human form,
In heathen, Turk, or Jew.
Where Mercy, Love, & Pity dwell,
There God is dwelling too.   20

---

clime: region
heathen: a person without religious convictions or faith

A Divine Image

Cruelty has a Human Heart
And Jealousy a Human Face,
Terror, the Human Form Divine,
And Secrecy, the Human Dress.

The Human Dress is forgèd Iron,   5
The Human Form, a fiery Forge,
The Human Face, a Furnace seal'd,
The Human Heart, its hungry Gorge.

---

forge: a workplace where metal is melted and shaped
gorge: the passage from the throat to the stomach

Infant Joy

"I have no name,
I am but two days old."
What shall I call thee?
"I happy am,
Joy is my name." 5
Sweet joy befall thee!

Pretty joy!
Sweet joy but two days old,
Sweet joy I call thee;
Thou dost smile, 10
I sing the while—
Sweet joy befall thee.

Infant Sorrow

My mother groand! my father wept.
Into the dangerous world I leapt,
Helpless, naked, piping loud;
Like a fiend hid in a cloud.

Struggling in my father's hands, 5
Striving against my swadling bands;
Bound and weary I thought best
To sulk upon my mother's breast.

---

befall: come to; happen; come to pass
groand: obsolete spelling of *groaned*
swadling bands: pieces of cloth wrapped around an infant
sulk: mope

I Wandered Lonely as a Cloud

William Wordsworth

William Wordsworth (1770–1850), one of the founders of the Romantic movement in poetry in England, often found inspiration in nature. This well-known poem is sometimes called "The Daffodils."

I wandered lonely as a cloud
That floats on high o'er vales and hills,
When all at once I saw a crowd,
A host, of golden daffodils;
Beside the lake, beneath the trees,　　　　　　　　5
Fluttering and dancing in the breeze.

Continuous as the stars that shine
And twinkle on the milky way,
They stretched in never-ending line
Along the margin of a bay:　　　　　　　　10
Ten thousand saw I at a glance,
Tossing their heads in sprightly dance.

---

vales: valleys
margin: edge; shore

The waves beside them danced; but they
Out-did the sparkling waves in glee:
A poet could not but be gay,   15
In such a jocund company:
I gazed—and gazed—but little thought
What wealth the show to me had brought:

For oft, when on my couch I lie
In vacant or in pensive mood,   20
They flash upon that inward eye
Which is the bliss of solitude;
And then my heart with pleasure fills,
And dances with the daffodils.

---

jocund: jovial; happy
pensive: thoughtful
bliss: great happiness; blessing

LINES WRITTEN IN EARLY SPRING

William Wordsworth

This poem first appeared in a 1798 volume titled Lyrical Ballads, *a book with works by both Wordsworth and his friend and fellow Romantic poet, Samuel Taylor Coleridge.*

I heard a thousand blended notes,
While in a grove I sate reclined,
In that sweet mood when pleasant thoughts
Bring sad thoughts to the mind.

To her fair works did Nature link   5
The human soul that through me ran;
And much it grieved my heart to think
What man has made of man.

Through primrose tufts, in that green bower,
The periwinkle trailed its wreaths;   10
And 'tis my faith that every flower
Enjoys the air it breathes.

---

grove: a wooded area
sate: obsolete form of *sat*
grieved: saddened
primrose tufts: bunches of a plant with white, red, or yellow
    flowers
bower: a place enclosed by tree branches or vines
periwinkle: a plant with blue flowers

The birds around me hopped and played,
Their thoughts I cannot measure:—
But the least motion which they made,   15
It seemed a thrill of pleasure.

The budding twigs spread out their fan,
To catch the breezy air;
And I must think, do all I can,
That there was pleasure there.   20

If this belief from heaven be sent,
If such be Nature's holy plan,
Have I not reason to lament
What man has made of man?

_____

lament: mourn; be sad over

KUBLA KHAN

OR, A VISION IN A DREAM. A FRAGMENT

Samuel Taylor Coleridge

With his friend and fellow poet William Wordsworth, Samuel Taylor Coleridge (1772–1834) was one of the founders of the Romantic movement in English poetry. Of the following poem, Coleridge said that, waking from "a profound sleep," he "instantly and eagerly wrote down the lines," only to be interrupted by "a person on business." More than an hour later, as he tried to resume writing, he found that the vision "had passed away like the images on the surface of a stream."

> In Xanadu did Kubla Khan
> A stately pleasure-dome decree:
> Where Alph, the sacred river, ran
> Through caverns measureless to man
>   Down to a sunless sea.   5
> So twice five miles of fertile ground
> With walls and towers were girdled round:
> And there were gardens bright with sinuous rills
> Where blossomed many an incense-bearing tree;
> And here were forests ancient as the hills,   10
> Enfolding sunny spots of greenery.

Xanadu: the luxurious summer capital of Kubla Khan's kingdom
Kubla Khan: a thirteenth-century ruler of the Mongols, who lived in
    what is now Mongolia and northwestern China
decree: order
Alph: a fictional river
girdled: encircled; ringed
sinuous rills: curved streams

But oh! that deep romantic chasm which slanted
Down the green hill athwart a cedarn cover!
A savage place! as holy and enchanted
As e'er beneath a waning moon was haunted   15
By woman wailing for her demon-lover!
And from this chasm, with ceaseless turmoil
    seething,
As if this earth in fast thick pants were breathing,
A mighty fountain momently was forced:
Amid whose swift half-intermitted burst   20
Huge fragments vaulted like rebounding hail,
Or chaffy grain beneath the thresher's flail:
And 'mid these dancing rocks at once and ever
It flung up momently the sacred river.
Five miles meandering with a mazy motion   25
Through wood and dale the sacred river ran,
Then reached the caverns measureless to man,
And sank in tumult to a lifeless ocean:
And 'mid this tumult Kubla heard from far
Ancestral voices prophesying war!   30

    The shadow of the dome of pleasure
    Floated midway on the waves;
    Where was heard the mingled measure
    From the fountain and the caves.
It was a miracle of rare device,   35
A sunny pleasure-dome with caves of ice!

---

athwart: diagonally across from
cedarn: made of cedar wood
turmoil: chaos; tumult
seething: moving as though furious
half-intermitted: half-interrupted
chaffy grain: the inedible part of grain
thresher's flail: the harvester's swinging motion
meandering: twisting
tumult: commotion; uproar
prophesying: predicting

A damsel with a dulcimer
In a vision once I saw:
It was an Abyssinian maid,
And on her dulcimer she played,   40
Singing of Mount Abora.
Could I revive within me
Her symphony and song,
To such a deep delight 'twould win me,
That with music loud and long,   45
I would build that dome in air,
That sunny dome! those caves of ice!
And all who heard should see them there,
And all should cry, Beware! Beware!
His flashing eyes, his floating hair!   50
Weave a circle round him thrice,
And close your eyes with holy dread,
For he on honey-dew hath fed,
And drunk the milk of Paradise.

---

dulcimer: a stringed instrument
Abyssinian: one from a region in Africa that is present-day Ethiopia
Mount Abora: perhaps Mount Amara in Abyssinia

WHEN WE TWO PARTED

George Gordon, Lord Byron

In his time, Lord Byron (1788–1824) was known the world over. He was both a poet and a celebrity, described by one French critic as "the model that contemporaries invest with their admiration and sympathy." His poetry, often marked by passionate feeling, captures one defining aspect of the Romantic temperament.

1

When we two parted
   In silence and tears,
Half broken-hearted
   To sever for years,
Pale grew thy cheek and cold,   5
   Colder thy kiss;
Truly that hour foretold
   Sorrow to this.

2

The dew of the morning
   Sunk chill on my brow—   10
It felt like the warning
   Of what I feel now.
Thy vows are all broken,
   And light is thy fame;
I hear thy name spoken,   15
   And share in its shame.

---

sever: separate; split
foretold: predicted

They name thee before me,
    A knell to mine ear;
A shudder comes o'er me—
    Why wert thou so dear?   20
They know not I knew thee,
    Who knew thee too well:—
Long, long shall I rue thee,
    Too deeply to tell.

4

In secret we met—   25
    In silence I grieve,
That thy heart could forget,
    Thy spirit deceive.
If I should meet thee
    After long years,   30
How should I greet thee?—
    With silence and tears.

---

knell: the sound of a bell tolled at a funeral
wert: obsolete form of *were*
rue: lament

Darkness

George Gordon, Lord Byron

Lord Byron's "Darkness" was published in 1816, known as the "year without a summer" because in the previous year a massive volcanic eruption in Indonesia altered the world's weather patterns. Byron's poetic imagination transformed these events into an apocalyptic vision of the end of life on earth.

I had a dream, which was not all a dream.
The bright sun was extinguish'd, and the stars
Did wander darkling in the eternal space,
Rayless, and pathless, and the icy earth
Swung blind and blackening in the moonless air;   5
Morn came, and went—and came, and brought
    no day,
And men forgot their passions in the dread
Of this their desolation; and all hearts
Were chill'd into a selfish prayer for light:
And they did live by watchfires—and the thrones,   10
The palaces of crowned kings—the huts,
The habitations of all things which dwell,
Were burnt for beacons; cities were consumed,
And men were gathered round their blazing
    homes
To look once more into each other's face;   15
Happy were those who dwelt within the eye
Of the volcanos, and their mountain-torch:
A fearful hope was all the world contain'd;
Forests were set on fire—but hour by hour
They fell and faded—and the crackling trunks   20
Extinguish'd with a crash—and all was black.

---

darkling: in the dark
beacons: fires used to aid people in navigation

The brows of men by the despairing light
Wore an unearthly aspect, as by fits
The flashes fell upon them; some lay down
And hid their eyes and wept; and some did rest   25
Their chins upon their clenched hands, and smiled;
And others hurried to and fro, and fed
Their funeral piles with fuel, and looked up
With mad disquietude on the dull sky,
The pall of a past world; and then again   30
With curses cast them down upon the dust,
And gnash'd their teeth and howl'd: the wild birds
    shriek'd,
And, terrified, did flutter on the ground,
And flap their useless wings; the wildest brutes
Came tame and tremulous; and vipers crawl'd   35
And twined themselves among the multitude,
Hissing, but stingless—they were slain for food:
And War, which for a moment was no more,
Did glut himself again;—a meal was bought
With blood, and each sate sullenly apart   40
Gorging himself in gloom: no love was left;
All earth was but one thought—and that was
    death,
Immediate and inglorious; and the pang
Of famine fed upon all entrails—men
Died, and their bones were tombless as their flesh;   45
The meagre by the meagre were devoured,
Even dogs assail'd their masters, all save one,
And he was faithful to a corse, and kept

---

disquietude: anxiety
pall: a burial cloth, used to cover a corpse or coffin
tremulous: shaking with fear
twined: intertwined
glut: feed ravenously
sate: obsolete form of *sat*
pang: sharp, sudden pain
entrails: intestines
assail'd: attacked
corse: obsolete word for *corpse*

The birds and beasts and famish'd men at bay,
Till hunger clung them, or the dropping dead   50
Lured their lank jaws; himself sought out no food,
But with a piteous and perpetual moan,
And a quick desolate cry, licking the hand
Which answered not with a caress—he died.
The crowd was famish'd by degrees; but two   55
Of an enormous city did survive,
And they were enemies; they met beside
The dying embers of an altar-place,
Where had been heap'd a mass of holy things
For an unholy usage; they raked up,   60
And shivering scraped with their cold skeleton
     hands
The feeble ashes, and their feeble breath
Blew for a little life, and made a flame
Which was a mockery; then they lifted up
Their eyes as it grew lighter, and beheld   65
Each other's aspects—saw, and shriek'd, and
     died—
Even of their mutual hideousness they died,
Unknowing who he was upon whose brow
Famine had written Fiend. The world was void,
The populous and the powerful—was a lump,   70
Seasonless, herbless, treeless, manless, lifeless—
A lump of death—a chaos of hard clay.
The rivers, lakes, and ocean all stood still,
And nothing stirred within their silent depths;
Ships sailorless lay rotting on the sea,   75
And their masts fell down piecemeal; as they
     dropp'd
They slept on the abyss without a surge—

---

lank: long and skinny; thinned
piteous: pathetic
aspects: faces
void: empty
piecemeal: piece by piece
abyss: a seemingly unending chasm

The waves were dead; the tides were in their grave,
The moon their mistress had expired before;
The winds were withered in the stagnant air,   80
And the clouds perish'd; Darkness had no need
Of aid from them—She was the universe.

---

stagnant: unmoving

ODE TO THE WEST WIND

Percy Bysshe Shelley

In his time, Shelley (1792–1822) was a controversial figure, both for his radical politics and his unconventional personal life. After marrying his second wife, Mary Wollstonecraft Godwin (the author of Frankenstein*), Shelley moved to Italy, where he wrote "Ode to the West Wind." About this ode (a lyric poem in high, formal style, with elaborate stanza forms), Shelley wrote: "This poem was conceived and chiefly written in a wood that skirts the Arno [River], near Florence, and on a day when that tempestuous wind, whose temperature is at once mild and animating, was collecting the vapors which pour down the autumnal rains."*

1

O wild West Wind, thou breath of Autumn's being,
Thou, from whose unseen presence the leaves dead
Are driven, like ghosts from an enchanter fleeing,

Yellow, and black, and pale, and hectic red,
Pestilence-stricken multitudes: O Thou,   5
Who chariotest to their dark wintry bed

The wingèd seeds, where they lie cold and low,
Each like a corpse within its grave, until
Thine azure sister of the Spring shall blow

---

pestilence-stricken: struck with disease
chariotest: transport
azure: a light shade of blue

Her clarion o'er the dreaming earth, and fill   10
(Driving sweet buds like flocks to feed in air)
With living hues and odours plain and hill:

Wild Spirit, which art moving everywhere;
Destroyer and Preserver; hear, O hear!

2

Thou on whose stream, 'mid the steep sky's   15
    commotion,
Loose clouds like Earth's decaying leaves are shed,
Shook from the tangled boughs of Heaven and Ocean,

Angels of rain and lightning: there are spread
On the blue surface of thine aery surge,
Like the bright hair uplifted from the head   20

Of some fierce Mænad, even from the dim verge
Of the horizon to the zenith's height,
The locks of the approaching storm. Thou Dirge

Of the dying year, to which this closing night
Will be the dome of a vast sepulchre,   25
Vaulted with all thy congregated might

Of vapours, from whose solid atmosphere
Black rain and fire and hail will burst: O hear!

---

clarion: a medieval brass instrument, like a trumpet, with a clear,
    piercing sound
hues: colors
Mænad: an ecstatic or extremely emotional woman (from Greek
    mythology, after the frenzied worshippers of Dionysus)
zenith: summit; highest point
dirge: a funeral hymn; a song of lamentation

3

Thou who didst waken from his summer dreams
The blue Mediterranean, where he lay,   30
Lulled by the coil of his chrystalline streams,

Beside a pumice isle in Baiæ's bay,
And saw in sleep old palaces and towers
Quivering within the wave's intenser day,

All overgrown with azure moss and flowers   35
So sweet, the sense faints picturing them! Thou
For whose path the Atlantic's level powers

Cleave themselves into chasms, while far below
The sea-blooms and the oozy woods which wear
The sapless foliage of the ocean, know   40

Thy voice, and suddenly grow grey with fear,
And tremble and despoil themselves: O hear!

4

If I were a dead leaf thou mightest bear;
If I were a swift cloud to fly with thee;
A wave to pant beneath thy power, and share   45

The impulse of thy strength, only less free
Than thou, O Uncontrollable! If even
I were as in my boyhood, and could be

---

chrystalline: clear or bright
pumice: a volcanic rock
Baiæ's bay: the Bay of Naples in Italy
quivering: trembling; shaking
cleave: slice; cut
despoil: defile; damage

The comrade of thy wanderings over Heaven,
As then, when to outstrip thy skiey speed   50
Scarce seemed a vision; I would ne'er have striven

As thus with thee in prayer in my sore need.
Oh! lift me as a wave, a leaf, a cloud!
I fall upon the thorns of life! I bleed!

A heavy weight of hours has chained and bowed   55
One too like thee: tameless, and swift, and proud.

5

Make me thy lyre, even as the forest is:
What if my leaves are falling like its own!
The tumult of thy mighty harmonies

Will take from both a deep, autumnal tone,   60
Sweet though in sadness. Be thou, Spirit fierce,
My spirit! Be thou me, impetuous one!

Drive my dead thoughts over the universe
Like withered leaves to quicken a new birth!
And, by the incantation of this verse,   65

Scatter, as from an unextinguished hearth
Ashes and sparks, my words among mankind!
Be through my lips to unawakened Earth

The trumpet of a prophecy! O Wind,
If Winter comes, can Spring be far behind?   70

---

outstrip: surpass
skiey: heavenly; resembling the sky
striven: attempted; tried
lyre: a harp
impetuous: impulsive; reckless
withered: shrunken
incantation: chant
hearth: a fireplace

La Belle Dame sans Merci: A Ballad

John Keats

John Keats (1795–1821) died of tuberculosis at the age of 25. In his short career, he produced a lasting and influential body of poetry that expresses the Romantic cultivation of deep and intense feeling. Keats wrote "La Belle Dame sans Merci" in 1819, but he took the title from a work by a fifteenth-century French poet. In English, the poem's title is "The Beautiful Woman Without Pity."

1

O what can ail thee, knight at arms,
    Alone and palely loitering?
The sedge has wither'd from the lake,
    And no birds sing.

2

O what can ail thee, knight at arms,   5
    So haggard and so woe-begone?
The squirrel's granary is full,
    And the harvest's done.

---

ail: sicken; make unwell or uneasy
loitering: waiting; lingering
sedge: a small, grassy plant that commonly grows in wet areas
wither'd: shriveled; shrunken
haggard: tired
woe-begone: miserably sad
granary: a structure for storing food

3

I see a lily on thy brow
    With anguish moist and fever dew,   10
And on thy cheeks a fading rose
    Fast withereth too.

4

I met a lady in the meads,
    Full beautiful, a fairy's child;
Her hair was long, her foot was light,   15
    And her eyes were wild.

5

I made a garland for her head,
    And bracelets too, and fragrant zone;
She look'd at me as she did love,
    And made sweet moan.   20

6

I set her on my pacing steed,
    And nothing else saw all day long,
For sidelong would she bend, and sing
    A fairy's song.

---

meads: meadows
garland: a wreath made of flowers or leaves
zone: a cincture or girdle; a band of material around the waist
steed: horse

7

She found me roots of relish sweet,   25
 And honey wild, and manna dew,
And sure in language strange she said—
 I love thee true.

8

She took me to her elfin grot,
 And there she wept, and sigh'd full sore, 30
And there I shut her wild wild eyes
 With kisses four.

9

And there she lulled me asleep,
 And there I dream'd—Ah! woe betide!
The latest dream I ever dream'd   35
 On the cold hill's side.

10

I saw pale kings, and princes too,
 Pale warriors, death pale were they all;
They cried—"La belle dame sans merci
 Hath thee in thrall!"   40

---

grot: grotto; a small cave
betide: happen to
in thrall: enslaved; in a state of servitude

11

I saw their starv'd lips in the gloam
    With horrid warning gaped wide,
And I awoke and found me here
    On the cold hill's side.

12

And this is why I sojourn here, 45
    Alone and palely loitering,
Though the sedge is wither'd from the lake,
    And no birds sing.

---

gloam: the twilight
sojourn: dwell temporarily

ODE ON MELANCHOLY

John Keats

Keats wrote his "Ode on Melancholy" in 1819. An ode is a lyric poem in a high, formal style, with elaborate stanza forms.

1

No, no, go not to Lethe, neither twist
    Wolf's-bane, tight-rooted, for its poisonous wine;
Nor suffer thy pale forehead to be kiss'd
    By nightshade, ruby grape of Proserpine;
Make not your rosary of yew-berries,   5
    Nor let the beetle, nor the death-moth be
        Your mournful Psyche, nor the downy owl
A partner in your sorrow's mysteries;
    For shade to shade will come too drowsily,
        And drown the wakeful anguish of the soul.   10

Lethe: in Greek mythology, one of the rivers that runs through the
    underworld, from which the souls of the dead drink in order to
    forget their past lives
wolf's-bane…nightshade: poisonous plants
Proserpine: in ancient Roman mythology, a woman abducted by
    Hades and made goddess of the underworld
Psyche: In ancient mythology, Psyche, or the soul, was sometimes
    represented as a butterfly or moth.
downy: covered in soft feathers

But when the melancholy fit shall fall
    Sudden from heaven like a weeping cloud,
That fosters the droop-headed flowers all,
    And hides the green hill in an April shroud;
Then glut thy sorrow on a morning rose,   15
    Or on the rainbow of the salt sand-wave,
      Or on the wealth of globed peonies;
Or if thy mistress some rich anger shows,
    Emprison her soft hand, and let her rave,
      And feed deep, deep upon her peerless eyes.   20

3

She dwells with Beauty—Beauty that must die;
    And Joy, whose hand is ever at his lips
Bidding adieu; and aching Pleasure nigh,
    Turning to poison while the bee-mouth sips:
Ay, in the very temple of Delight   25
    Veil'd Melancholy has her sovran shrine,
      Though seen of none save him whose
           strenuous tongue
    Can burst Joy's grape against his palate fine;
His soul shall taste the sadness of her might,
    And be among her cloudy trophies hung.   30

---

fosters: aids
glut: feed ravenously; flood
peonies: large, fragrant flowers
emprison: obsolete spelling of *imprison*
adieu: farewell
nigh: near
sovran: obsolete spelling of *sovereign*
strenuous: demanding

The Modern Age

THE SECOND COMING

W.B. Yeats

*The Irish poet and playwright W.B. Yeats (1865–1939) published this
poem in 1920, as Europe was emerging from the brutality and devastation
of World War I.*

Turning and turning in the widening gyre
The falcon cannot hear the falconer;
Things fall apart; the center cannot hold;
Mere anarchy is loosed upon the world,
The blood-dimmed tide is loosed, and everywhere   5
The ceremony of innocence is drowned;
The best lack all conviction, while the worst
Are full of passionate intensity.
Surely some revelation is at hand;
Surely the Second Coming is at hand.   10
The Second Coming! Hardly are those words out
When a vast image out of *Spiritus Mundi*
Troubles my sight: somewhere in sands of the desert
A shape with lion body and the head of a man,
A gaze blank and pitiless as the sun,   15
Is moving its slow thighs, while all about it
Reel shadows of the indignant desert birds.
The darkness drops again; but now I know
That twenty centuries of stony sleep
Were vexed to nightmare by a rocking cradle,   20
And what rough beast, its hour come round at last,
Slouches towards Bethlehem to be born?

---

gyre: a round swirling shape; a conical vortex
anarchy: a state of lawlessness and social disorder
Second Coming: in Christian theology, the return of Christ to earth
Spiritus Mundi: Latin for "spirit of the world"
vexed: angered; disturbed

AN IRISH AIRMAN FORESEES HIS DEATH

W.B. Yeats

*This is one of four poems that Yeats wrote about Major Robert Gregory,
an accomplished painter and the only son of Yeats's literary benefactor,
Lady August Gregory. Major Gregory died in 1918 while fighting in
World War I.*

I know that I shall meet my fate
Somewhere among the clouds above;
Those that I fight I do not hate,
Those that I guard I do not love;
My country is Kiltartan Cross,   5
My countrymen Kiltartan's poor,
No likely end could bring them loss
Or leave them happier than before.
Nor law, nor duty bade me fight,
Nor public men, nor cheering crowds,   10
A lonely impulse of delight
Drove to this tumult in the clouds;
I balanced all, brought all to mind,
The years to come seemed waste of breath,
A waste of breath the years behind   15
In balance with this life, this death.

---

bade: past tense of *bid*; commanded
tumult: commotion; agitation; uproar

THE LOVE SONG OF J. ALFRED PRUFROCK

T.S. Eliot

T.S. (Thomas Stearns) Eliot (1888–1965) was born in St. Louis, but lived most of his life in London, and became a British citizen. "The Love Song of J. Alfred Prufrock," first published in 1915 in Poetry *magazine, is considered by many as the first masterpiece of modernism in English poetry. The poem takes the form of a dramatic monologue, expressing the thoughts and observations of the middle-aged speaker. Like much of Eliot's work, "Prufrock" is full of learned allusions and references. "The poet," Eliot once wrote," must become more and more comprehensive, more allusive, more indirect, in order to force, to dislocate if necessary, language into his meaning."*

> *S'io credesse che mia risposta fosse*
> *a persona che mai tornasse al mondo,*
> *questa fiamma staria senza più scosse.*
> *Ma perciocche giammai di questo fondo*
> *non torno vivo alcun, s'i'odo il vero,*
> *senza tema d'infamia ti rispondo.*

Let us go then, you and I,
When the evening is spread out against the sky
Like a patient etherised upon a table;
Let us go, through certain half-deserted streets,
The muttering retreats   5
Of restless nights in one-night cheap hotels
And sawdust restaurants with oyster shells:

S'io credesse che mia...ti rispondo: The epigraph, from the *Inferno* by
    Dante (1265–1321), is spoken by a condemned soul enclosed in
    flame, who says, "If I thought my reply were to one who ever
    could return unto the world, this flame would rest unshaken.
    But since, if what I am told is true, none has ever returned alive
    from this depth, then without fear of infamy I answer you."
etherised: anesthetized; drugged and put to sleep

Streets that follow like a tedious argument
Of insidious intent
To lead you to an overwhelming question…   10
Oh, do not ask, 'What is it?'
Let us go and make our visit.

In the room the women come and go
Talking of Michelangelo.

The yellow fog that rubs its back upon the
    window-panes,   15
The yellow smoke that rubs its muzzle on the
    window-panes
Licked its tongue into the corners of the evening,
Lingered upon the pools that stand in drains,
Let fall upon its back the soot that falls from
    chimneys,
Slipped by the terrace, made a sudden leap,   20
And seeing that it was a soft October night,
Curled once about the house, and fell asleep.

And indeed there will be time
For the yellow smoke that slides along the street,
Rubbing its back upon the window-panes;   25
There will be time, there will be time
To prepare a face to meet the faces that you meet;
There will be time to murder and create,
And time for all the works and days of hands
That lift and drop a question on your plate;   30
Time for you and time for me,
And time yet for a hundred indecisions,
And for a hundred visions and revisions,
Before the taking of a toast and tea.

---

tedious: tiresome
insidious: sinister; menacing
Michelangelo: a master painter, sculptor, and architect of the Italian
    Renaissance
muzzle: snout

In the room the women come and go   35
Talking of Michelangelo.

And indeed there will be time
To wonder, 'Do I dare?' and, 'Do I dare?'
Time to turn back and descend the stair,
With a bald spot in the middle of my hair—   40
(They will say: 'How his hair is growing thin!')
My morning coat, my collar mounting firmly to
    the chin,
My necktie rich and modest, but asserted by a
    simple pin—
(They will say: 'But how his arms and legs are thin!')
Do I dare   45
Disturb the universe?
In a minute there is time
For decisions and revisions which a minute will
    reverse.

For I have known them all already, known
    them all—
Have known the evenings, mornings, afternoons,   50
I have measured out my life with coffee spoons;
I know the voices dying with a dying fall
Beneath the music from a farther room.
So how should I presume?

And I have known the eyes already, known   55
    them all—
The eyes that fix you in a formulated phrase,
And when I am formulated, sprawling on a pin,
When I am pinned and wriggling on the wall,
Then how should I begin
To spit out all the butt-ends of my days and ways?   60
    And how should I presume?

And I have known the arms already, known
    them all—

Arms that are braceleted and white and bare
(But in the lamplight, downed with light brown
    hair!)
Is it perfume from a dress   65
That makes me so digress?
Arms that lie along a table, or wrap about a shawl.
    And should I then presume?
    And how should I begin?

• • •

Shall I say, I have gone at dusk through narrow   70
    streets
And watched the smoke that rises from the pipes
Of lonely men in shirt-sleeves, leaning out of
    windows?…

I should have been a pair of ragged claws
Scuttling across the floors of silent seas.

• • •

And the afternoon, the evening, sleeps so   75
    peacefully!
Smoothed by long fingers,
Asleep…tired…or it malingers,
Stretched on the floor, here beside you and me.
Should I, after tea and cakes and ices,
Have the strength to force the moment to its crisis? 80
But though I have wept and fasted, wept and
    prayed,

---

digress: to stray; to turn aside from the main point in writing or
    speaking
scuttling: scurrying; shuffling
malingers: fakes a disease or an injury in order to avoid
    responsibility or work

Though I have seen my head (grown slightly bald)
     brought in upon a platter,
I am no prophet—and here's no great matter;
I have seen the moment of my greatness flicker,
And I have seen the eternal Footman hold my coat,   85
     and snicker,
And in short, I was afraid.

And would it have been worth it, after all,
After the cups, the marmalade, the tea,
Among the porcelain, among some talk of you and me,
Would it have been worth while,   90
To have bitten off the matter with a smile,
To have squeezed the universe into a ball
To roll it toward some overwhelming question,
To say: 'I am Lazarus, come from the dead,
Come back to tell you all, I shall tell you all'—   95
If one, settling a pillow by her head,
     Should say: 'That is not what I meant at all.
     That is not it, at all.'

And would it have been worth it, after all,
Would it have been worth while,   100
After the sunsets and the dooryards and the
     sprinkled streets,
After the novels, after the teacups, after the skirts
     that trail along the floor—
And this, and so much more?—
It is impossible to say just what I mean!
But as if a magic lantern threw the nerves in   105
     patterns on a screen:
Would it have been worth while
If one, settling a pillow or throwing off a shawl,

---

head…brought in upon a platter: as happened to John the Baptist,
     according to accounts in the Bible
footman: butler; male domestic servant
Lazarus: in the Bible, a man who was miraculously raised from the
     dead by Christ

And turning toward the window, should say:
    'That is not it at all,
    That is not what I meant, at all.'   110

• • •

No! I am not Prince Hamlet, nor was meant to be;
Am an attendant lord, one that will do
To swell a progress, start a scene or two,
Advise the prince; no doubt, an easy tool,
Deferential, glad to be of use,   115
Politic, cautious, and meticulous;
Full of high sentence, but a bit obtuse;
At times, indeed, almost ridiculous—
Almost, at times, the Fool.

I grow old...I grow old...   120
I shall wear the bottoms of my trousers rolled.

Shall I part my hair behind? Do I dare to eat a peach?
I shall wear white flannel trousers, and walk upon
    the beach.
I have heard the mermaids singing, each to each.

I do not think that they will sing to me.   125

I have seen them riding seaward on the waves
Combing the white hair of the waves blown back
When the wind blows the water white and black.

We have lingered in the chambers of the sea
By sea-girls wreathed with seaweed red and brown 130
Till human voices wake us, and we drown.

Prince Hamlet: central figure of William Shakespeare's play *Hamlet*,
    known for being both thoughtful and indecisive
deferential: respectful
meticulous: extremely careful and thorough
obtuse: insensitive; slow to understand

Do Not Go Gentle into That Good Night

Dylan Thomas

The Welsh writer Dylan Thomas: (1914–1953) wrote "Do Not Go Gentle into That Good Night" in 1952 for his dying father. The poem is in the form of a villanelle, *a 19-line poem consisting of five three-line stanzas and a concluding quatrain (four-line stanza).*

Do not go gentle into that good night,
Old age should burn and rave at close of day;
Rage, rage against the dying of the light.

Though wise men at their end know dark is right,
Because their words had forked no lightning they   5
Do not go gentle into that good night.

Good men, the last wave by, crying how bright
Their frail deeds might have danced in a green bay,
Rage, rage against the dying of the light.

Wild men who caught and sang the sun in flight,   10
And learn, too late, they grieved it on its way,
Do not go gentle into that good night.

Grave men, near death, who see with blinding sight
Blind eyes could blaze like meteors and be gay,
Rage, rage against the dying of the light.   15

And you, my father, there on the sad height,
Curse, bless, me now with your fierce tears, I pray.
Do not go gentle into that good night.
Rage, rage against the dying of the light.

EVELINE

James Joyce

As a young man, James Joyce: (1882–1941) left the city of his birth, Dublin, Ireland. But throughout his career, Joyce continued to set his writings—including the radically experimental novel Ulysses *(1922)—in his native city. "Eveline" is from his 1914 collection of stories,* Dubliners.

She sat at the window watching the evening invade the avenue. Her head was leaned against the window curtains and in her nostrils was the odour of dusty cretonne. She was tired.

Few people passed. The man out of the last house passed on his way home; she heard his footsteps clacking along the concrete pavement and afterwards crunching on the cinder path before the new red houses. One time there used to be a field there in which they used to play every evening with other people's children. Then a man from Belfast bought the field and built houses in it—not like their little brown houses but bright brick houses with shining roofs. The children of the avenue used to play together in that field—the Devines, the Waters, the Dunns, little Keogh the cripple, she and her brothers and sisters. Ernest, however, never played: he was too grown up. Her father used often to hunt them in out of the field with his blackthorn stick; but usually little Keogh used to keep *nix* and call out when he saw her father coming. Still they seemed to have been rather happy then. Her father was not so bad then; and besides, her mother was alive. That was a long time ago; she and her brothers and sisters were all grown up; her mother was dead. Tizzie Dunn was dead, too, and the Waters had gone back to

---

cretonne: a strong, heavy fabric
cinder: pebble
Belfast: the largest city in Northern Ireland
blackthorn stick: a walking stick
nix: guard

England. Everything changes. Now she was going to go away like the others, to leave her home.

Home! She looked round the room, reviewing all its familiar objects which she had dusted once a week for so many years, wondering where on earth all the dust came from. Perhaps she would never see again those familiar objects from which she had never dreamed of being divided. And yet during all those years she had never found out the name of the priest whose yellowing photograph hung on the wall above the broken harmonium beside the coloured print of the promises made to Blessed Margaret Mary Alacoque. He had been a school friend of her father. Whenever he showed the photograph to a visitor her father used to pass it with a casual word:

—He is in Melbourne now.

She had consented to go away, to leave her home. Was that wise? She tried to weigh each side of the question. In her home anyway she had shelter and food; she had those whom she had known all her life about her. Of course she had to work hard both in the house and at business. What would they say of her in the Stores when they found out that she had run away with a fellow? Say she was a fool, perhaps; and her place would be filled up by advertisement. Miss Gavan would be glad. She had always had an edge on her, especially whenever there were people listening.

—Miss Hill, don't you see these ladies are waiting?

—Look lively, Miss Hill, please.

She would not cry many tears at leaving the Stores.

But in her new home, in a distant unknown country, it would not be like that. Then she would be married—she, Eveline. People would treat her with respect then. She would not be treated as her mother had been. Even now, though she was over nineteen, she sometimes felt herself in danger of her father's violence. She knew it was that that had given her the palpitations. When they were growing up he had never gone for her, like he used to go for

---

harmonium: a musical instrument similar to a small organ
Blessed Margaret Mary Alacoque: a seventeenth-century French saint
Melbourne: a large city in Australia
in the Stores: in the store where Eveline works
the palpitations: rapid, irregular beating of the heart

Harry and Ernest, because she was a girl; but latterly he had begun to threaten her and say what he would do to her only for her dead mother's sake. And now she had nobody to protect her. Ernest was dead and Harry, who was in the church decorating business, was nearly always down somewhere in the country. Besides, the invariable squabble for money on Saturday nights had begun to weary her unspeakably. She always gave her entire wages—seven shillings—and Harry always sent up what he could but the trouble was to get any money from her father. He said she used to squander the money, that she had no head, that he wasn't going to give her his hard-earned money to throw about the streets, and much more, for he was usually fairly bad of a Saturday night. In the end he would give her the money and ask her had she any intention of buying Sunday's dinner. Then she had to rush out as quickly as she could and do her marketing, holding her black leather purse tightly in her hand as she elbowed her way through the crowds and returning home late under her load of provisions. She had hard work to keep the house together and to see that the two young children who had been left to her charge went to school regularly and got their meals regularly. It was hard work—a hard life—but now that she was about to leave it she did not find it a wholly undesirable life.

She was about to explore another life with Frank. Frank was very kind, manly, open-hearted. She was to go away with him by the night-boat to be his wife and to live with him in Buenos Aires where he had a home waiting for her. How well she remembered the first time she had seen him; he was lodging in a house on the main road where she used to visit. It seemed a few weeks ago. He was standing at the gate, his peaked cap pushed back on his head

---

latterly: recently
invariable: usual; unchanging
seven shillings: a relatively small amount of money
squander: waste
fairly bad: rather drunk
provisions: food and supplies
the night-boat: the evening ferry to Liverpool, England, from where ships set out
    for longer journeys
Buenos Aires: the capital of Argentina, in South America
peaked cap: a hat with a round top and a flat visor, like those often worn by police
    officers and soldiers

and his hair tumbled forward over a face of bronze. Then they had come to know each other. He used to meet her outside the Stores every evening and see her home. He took her to see *The Bohemian Girl* and she felt elated as she sat in an unaccustomed part of the theatre with him. He was awfully fond of music and sang a little. People knew that they were courting and, when he sang about the lass that loves a sailor, she always felt pleasantly confused. He used to call her Poppens out of fun. First of all it had been an excitement for her to have a fellow and then she had begun to like him. He had tales of distant countries. He had started as a deck boy at a pound a month on a ship of the Allan Line going out to Canada. He told her the names of the ships he had been on and the names of the different services. He had sailed through the Straits of Magellan and he told her stories of the terrible Patagonians. He had fallen on his feet in Buenos Ayres, he said, and had come over to the old country just for a holiday. Of course, her father had found out the affair and had forbidden her to have anything to say to him.

—I know these sailor chaps, he said.

One day he had quarrelled with Frank and after that she had to meet her lover secretly.

The evening deepened in the avenue. The white of two letters in her lap grew indistinct. One was to Harry; the other was to her father. Ernest had been her favourite but she liked Harry too. Her father was becoming old lately, she noticed; he would miss her. Sometimes he could be very nice. Not long before, when she had been laid up for a day, he had read her out a ghost story and made toast for her at the fire. Another day, when their mother was alive,

---

The Bohemian Girl: a popular nineteenth-century opera
elated: extremely happy
lass: young girl
Allan Line: a shipping line with boats that traveled from Liverpool, England, to the west coast of North America by sailing around the southern tip of South America
Straits of Magellan: a South American waterway that serves as a natural passage from the Atlantic to the Pacific Ocean through the southern tip of Chile
Patagonians: people from the Patagonia region of South America who, according to some European legends, were fierce giants
indistinct: blurry; unclear

they had all gone for a picnic to the Hill of Howth. She remembered her father putting on her mother's bonnet to make the children laugh.

Her time was running out but she continued to sit by the window, leaning her head against the window curtain, inhaling the odour of dusty cretonne. Down far in the avenue she could hear a street organ playing. She knew the air. Strange that it should come that very night to remind her of the promise to her mother, her promise to keep the home together as long as she could. She remembered the last night of her mother's illness; she was again in the close dark room at the other side of the hall and outside she heard a melancholy air of Italy. The organ-player had been ordered to go away and given sixpence. She remembered her father strutting back into the sickroom saying:

—Damned Italians! coming over here!

As she mused the pitiful vision of her mother's life laid its spell on the very quick of her being—that life of commonplace sacrifices closing in final craziness. She trembled as she heard again her mother's voice saying constantly with foolish insistence:

—Derevaun Seraun! Derevaun Seraun!

She stood up in a sudden impulse of terror. Escape! She must escape! Frank would save her. He would give her life, perhaps love, too. But she wanted to live. Why should she be unhappy? She had a right to happiness. Frank would take her in his arms, fold her in his arms. He would save her.

• • •

She stood among the swaying crowd in the station at the North Wall. He held her hand and she knew that he was speaking to her, saying something about the passage over and over again. The

---

Hill of Howth: a hill on a coastal peninsula just north of the city of Dublin
air: melody; song
sixpence: a small amount of money; loose change
mused: contemplated
Derevaun Seraun: the meaning is uncertain, though some scholars think it might be
    a garbled form of an old phrase meaning "the end of pleasure is pain"
the North Wall: a dock on the north bank of the River Liffey in Dublin, from which
    ferries departed

station was full of soldiers with brown baggages. Through the wide doors of the sheds she caught a glimpse of the black mass of the boat, lying in beside the quay wall, with illumined portholes. She answered nothing. She felt her cheek pale and cold and, out of a maze of distress, she prayed to God to direct her, to show her what was her duty. The boat blew a long mournful whistle into the mist. If she went, to-morrow she would be on the sea with Frank, steaming toward Buenos Ayres. Their passage had been booked. Could she still draw back after all he had done for her? Her distress awoke a nausea in her body and she kept moving her lips in silent fervent prayer.

A bell clanged upon her heart. She felt him seize her hand:

—Come!

All the seas of the world tumbled about her heart. He was drawing her into them: he would drown her. She gripped with both hands at the iron railing.

—Come!

No! No! No! It was impossible. Her hands clutched the iron in frenzy. Amid the seas she sent a cry of anguish!

—Eveline! Evvy!

He rushed beyond the barrier and called to her to follow. He was shouted at to go on but he still called to her. She set her white face to him, passive, like a helpless animal. Her eyes gave him no sign of love or farewell or recognition.

---

quay: a wharf on a riverside
illumined: lit
fervent: passionate
passive: inactive

THE LADY IN THE LOOKING GLASS

Virginia Woolf

Virginia Woolf (1882–1941) is best known for her novels, in which she experimented with the presentation of time and character in ways that influenced many modern writers. Her innovative short story, "The Lady in the Looking Glass," was first published in 1929.

People should not leave looking glasses hanging in their rooms any more than they should leave open checkbooks or letters confessing some hideous crime. One could not help looking, that summer afternoon, in the long glass that hung outside in the hall. Chance had so arranged it. From the depths of the sofa in the drawing room one could see reflected in the Italian glass not only the marble-topped table opposite, but a stretch of the garden beyond. One could see a long grass path leading between banks of tall flowers until, slicing off an angle, the gold rim cut it off.

The house was empty, and one felt, since one was the only person in the drawing room, like one of those naturalists who, covered with grass and leaves, lie watching the shyest animals— badgers, otters, king-fishers—moving about freely, themselves unseen. The room that afternoon was full of such shy creatures, lights and shadows, curtains blowing, petals falling—things that never happen, so it seems, if someone is looking. The quiet old country room with its rugs and stone chimney pieces, its sunken bookcases and red and gold lacquer cabinets, was full of such nocturnal creatures. They came pirouetting across the floor, step-ping delicately with high-lifted feet and spread tails and pecking allusive beaks as if they had been cranes or flocks of elegant flamin-goes whose pink was faded, or peacocks whose trains were veiled

---

lacquer: a hard, glossy coating or varnish
pirouetting: spinning
allusive: meaningful

with silver. And there were obscure flushes and darkening too, as if a cuttlefish had suddenly suffused the air with purple; and the room had its passions and rages and envies and sorrows coming over it and clouding it, like a human being. Nothing stayed the same for two seconds together.

But, outside, the looking glass reflected the hall table, the sunflowers, the garden path so accurately and so fixedly that they seemed held there in their reality unescapably. It was a strange contrast—all changing here, all stillness there. One could not help looking from one to the other. Meanwhile, since all the doors and windows were open in the heat, there was a perpetual sighing and ceasing sound, the voice of the transient and the perishing, it seemed, coming and going like human breath, while in the looking glass things had ceased to breathe and lay still in the trance of immortality.

Half an hour ago the mistress of the house, Isabella Tyson, had gone down the grass path in her thin summer dress, carrying a basket, and had vanished, sliced off by the gilt rim of the looking glass. She had gone presumably into the lower garden to pick flowers; or as it seemed more natural to suppose, to pick something light and fantastic and leafy and trailing, traveler's-joy, or one of those elegant sprays of convolvulus that twine round ugly walls and burst here and there into white and violet blossoms. She suggested the fantastic and the tremulous convolvulus rather than the upright aster, the starched zinnia, or her own burning roses alight like lamps on the straight posts of their rose trees. The comparison showed how very little, after all these years, one knew about her; for it is impossible that any woman of flesh and blood of fifty-five or

---

cuttlefish: a marine animal that, like its relatives the squid and the octopus, produces ink
suffused: thoroughly covered or filled, as with a liquid
perpetual: unending
transient: fleeting; temporary
gilt: gold-coated
traveler's-joy: a fragrant green and white flower
convolvulus: a flowering plant of the morning-glory family
tremulous: quivering; trembling
aster: a daisy-like flower
zinnia: a brightly colored flower

sixty should be really a wreath or a tendril. Such comparisons are worse than idle and superficial—they are cruel even, for they come like the convolvulus itself trembling between one's eyes and the truth. There must be truth; there must be a wall. Yet it was strange that after knowing her all these years one could not say what the truth about Isabella was; one still made up phrases like this about convolvulus and traveler's-joy. As for facts, it was a fact that she was a spinster; that she was rich; that she had bought this house and collected with her own hands—often in the most obscure corners of the world and at great risk from poisonous stings and Oriental diseases—the rugs, the chairs, the cabinets which now lived their nocturnal life before one's eyes. Sometimes it seemed as if they knew more about her than we, who sat on them, wrote at them, and trod on them so carefully, were allowed to know. In each of these cabinets were many little drawers, and each almost certainly held letters, tied with bows of ribbon, sprinkled with sticks of lavender or rose leaves. For it was another fact—if facts were what one wanted—that Isabella had known many people, had had many friends; and thus if one had the audacity to open a drawer and read her letters, one would find the traces of many agitations, of appointments to meet, of upbraidings for not having met, long letters of intimacy and affection, violent letters of jealousy and reproach, terrible final words of parting—for all those interviews and assignations had led to nothing—that is, she had never married, and yet, judging from the masklike indifference of her face, she had gone through twenty times more of passion and experience than those whose loves are trumpeted forth for all the world to hear. Under the stress of thinking about Isabella, her room became more shadowy and symbolic; the corners seemed darker, the legs of chairs and tables more spindly and hieroglyphic.

---

tendril: a thin stem of a plant
spinster: an elderly unmarried woman
audacity: boldness
agitations: disturbances
upbraidings: scoldings
reproach: criticism
assignations: secret meetings between lovers
hieroglyphic: pictorially symbolic, as the writings of the ancient Egyptians

Suddenly these reflections were ended violently and yet without a sound. A large black form loomed into the looking glass; blotted out everything, strewed the table with a packet of marble tablets veined with pink and gray, and was gone. But the picture was entirely altered. For the moment it was unrecognizable and irrational and entirely out of focus. One could not relate these tablets to any human purpose. And then by degrees some logical process set to work on them and began ordering and arranging them and bringing them into the fold of common experience. One realized at last that they were merely letters. The man had brought the post.

There they lay on the marble-topped table, all dripping with light and color at first and crude and unabsorbed. And then it was strange to see how they were drawn in and arranged and composed and made part of the picture and granted that stillness and immortality which the looking glass conferred. They lay there invested with a new reality and significance and with a greater heaviness, too, as if it would have needed a chisel to dislodge them from the table. And, whether it was fancy or not, they seemed to have become not merely a handful of casual letters but to be tablets graven with eternal truth—if one could read them, one would know everything there was to be known about Isabella, yes, and about life, too. The pages inside those marble-looking envelopes must be cut deep and scored thick with meaning. Isabella would come in, and take them, one by one, very slowly, and open them, and read them carefully word by word, and then with a profound sigh of comprehension, as if she had seen to the bottom of everything, she would tear the envelopes to little bits and tie the letters together and lock the cabinet drawer in her determination to conceal what she did not wish to be known.

The thought served as a challenge. Isabella did not wish to be known—but she should no longer escape. It was absurd, it was monstrous. If she concealed so much and knew so much one must prize her open with the first tool that came to hand—the imagination. One must fix one's mind upon her at that very moment.

---

graven: engraved
scored: etched
prize: to pry; to force open

One must fasten her down there. One must refuse to be put off any longer with sayings and doings such as the moment brought forth—with dinners and visits and polite conversations. One must put oneself in her shoes. If one took the phrase literally, it was easy to see the shoes in which she stood, down in the lower garden, at this moment. They were very narrow and long and fashionable— they were made of the softest and most flexible leather. Like everything she wore, they were exquisite. And she would be standing under the high hedge in the lower part of the garden, raising the scissors that were tied to her waist to cut some dead flower, some overgrown branch. The sun would beat down on her face, into her eyes; but no, at the critical moment a veil of cloud covered the sun, making the expression of her eyes doubtful—was it mocking or tender, brilliant or dull? One could only see the inde- terminate outline of her rather faded, fine face looking at the sky. She was thinking, perhaps, that she must order a new net for the strawberries; that she must send flowers to Johnson's widow; that it was time she drove over to see the Hippesleys in their new house. Those were the things she talked about at dinner certainly. But one was tired of the things that she talked about at dinner. It was her profounder state of being that one wanted to catch and turn to words, the state that is to the mind what breathing is to the body, what one calls happiness or unhappiness. At the mention of those words it became obvious, surely, that she must be happy. She was rich; she was distinguished; she had many friends; she traveled— she bought rugs in Turkey and blue pots in Persia. Avenues of pleasure radiated this way and that from where she stood with her scissors raised to cut the trembling branches while the lacy clouds veiled her face.

Here with a quick movement of her scissors she snipped the spray of traveler's-joy and it fell to the ground. As it fell, surely some light came in too, surely one could penetrate a little farther into her being. Her mind then was filled with tenderness and regret…. To cut an overgrown branch saddened her because it had once lived, and life was dear to her. Yes, and at the same time the fall of the branch would suggest to her how she must die herself

---

indeterminate: uncertain; imprecise

and all the futility and evanescence of things. And then again quickly catching this thought up, with her instant good sense, she thought life had treated her well; even if fall she must, it was to lie on the earth and molder sweetly into the roots of violets. So she stood thinking. Without making any thought precise—for she was one of those reticent people whose minds hold their thoughts enmeshed in clouds of silence—she was filled with thoughts. Her mind was like her room, in which lights advanced and retreated, came pirouetting and stepping delicately, spread their tails, pecked their way; and then her whole being was suffused, like the room again, with a cloud of some profound knowledge, some unspoken regret, and then she was full of locked drawers, stuffed with letters, like her cabinets. To talk of "prizing her open" as if she were an oyster, to use any but the finest and subtlest and most pliable tools upon her was impious and absurd. One must imagine—here was she in the looking glass. It made one start.

She was so far off at first that one could not see her clearly. She came lingering and pausing, here straightening a rose, there lifting a pink to smell it, but she never stopped; and all the time she became larger and larger in the looking glass, more and more completely the person into whose mind one had been trying to penetrate. One verified her by degrees—fitted the qualities one had discovered into this visible body. There were her gray-green dress, and her long shoes, her basket, and something sparkling at her throat. She came so gradually that she did not seem to derange the pattern in the glass, but only to bring in some new element which gently moved and altered the other objects as if asking them, courteously, to make room for her. And the letters and the table and the grass walk and the sunflowers which had been waiting in the looking glass separated and opened out so that she might be received among them. At last there she was, in the hall. She stopped dead. She stood by the table. She stood perfectly still. At once the looking glass began to pour over her a light that seemed to fix her; that seemed like some acid to bite off the unessential

evanescence: transience; temporary nature
reticent: reserved; quiet
pliable: workable
impious: disrespectful; immoral

and superficial and to leave only the truth. It was an enthralling spectacle. Everything dropped from her—clouds, dress, basket, diamond—all that one had called the creeper and convolvulus. Here was the hard wall beneath. Here was the woman herself. She stood naked in that pitiless light. And there was nothing. Isabella was perfectly empty. She had no thoughts. She had no friends. She cared for nobody. As for her letters, they were all bills. Look, as she stood there, old and angular, veined and lined, with her high nose and her wrinkled neck, she did not even trouble to open them.

People should not leave looking glasses hanging in their rooms.

---

enthralling: exciting and captivating

Cultures in Conflict

SHOOTING AN ELEPHANT

George Orwell

George Orwell (1903–1950) was the pseudonym of Eric Arthur Blair, a twentieth-century English author best known for his novels Animal Farm *and* Nineteen Eighty-Four. *The autobiographical essay that follows is based in part on Orwell's experiences as a colonial police officer in Burma in the 1920s.*

In Moulmein, in Lower Burma, I was hated by large numbers of people—the only time in my life that I have been important enough for this to happen to me. I was sub-divisional police officer of the town, and in an aimless, petty kind of way anti-European feeling was very bitter. No one had the guts to raise a riot, but if a European woman went through the bazaars alone somebody would probably spit betel juice over her dress. As a police officer I was an obvious target and was baited whenever it seemed safe to do so. When a nimble Burman tripped me up on the football field and the referee (another Burman) looked the other way, the crowd yelled with hideous laughter. This happened more than once. In the end the sneering yellow faces of young men that met me everywhere, the insults hooted after me when I was at a safe distance, got badly on my nerves. The young Buddhist priests were the worst of all. There were several thousands of them in the town and none of them seemed to have anything to do except stand on street corners and jeer at Europeans.

Burma: now Myanmar, a country in Southeast Asia that borders the Bay of Bengal
bazaars: shopping areas or marketplaces
betel juice: saliva resulting from chewing the leaves of the betel plant
baited: lured into a fight

All this was perplexing and upsetting. For at that time I had already made up my mind that imperialism was an evil thing and the sooner I chucked up my job and got out of it the better. Theoretically—and secretly, of course—I was all for the Burmese and all against their oppressors, the British. As for the job I was doing, I hated it more bitterly than I can perhaps make clear. In a job like that you see the dirty work of Empire at close quarters. The wretched prisoners huddling in the stinking cages of the lock-ups, the grey, cowed faces of the long-term convicts, the scarred buttocks of the men who had been flogged with bamboos—all these oppressed me with an intolerable sense of guilt. But I could get nothing into perspective. I was young and ill-educated and I had had to think out my problems in the utter silence that is imposed on every Englishman in the East. I did not even know that the British Empire is dying, still less did I know that it is a great deal better than the younger empires that are going to supplant it. All I knew was that I was stuck between my hatred of the empire I served and my rage against the evil-spirited little beasts who tried to make my job impossible. With one part of my mind I thought of the British Raj as an unbreakable tyranny, as something clamped down, *in saecula saeculorum*, upon the will of prostrate peoples; with another part I thought that the greatest joy in the world would be to drive a bayonet into a Buddhist priest's guts. Feelings like these are the normal by-products of imperialism; ask any Anglo-Indian official, if you can catch him off duty.

One day something happened which in a roundabout way was enlightening. It was a tiny incident in itself, but it gave me a better glimpse than I had had before of the real nature of imperialism— the real motives for which despotic governments act. Early one

---

perplexing: confusing
imperialism: empire building; the policy or action by which one country controls
    another country or territory
cowed: frightened and intimidated
flogged: beaten
imposed: forced
British Raj: British rule in India and Southeast Asia
in saecula saeculorum: Latin phrase meaning "forever and ever"
prostrate: lying face downward
despotic: tyrannical

morning the sub-inspector at a police station the other end of the
town rang me up on the phone and said that an elephant was
ravaging the bazaar. Would I please come and do something about
it? I did not know what I could do, but I wanted to see what was
happening and I got on to a pony and started out. I took my rifle,
an old .44 Winchester and much too small to kill an elephant, but
I thought the noise might be useful *in terrorem*. Various Burmans
stopped me on the way and told me about the elephant's doings.
It was not, of course, a wild elephant, but a tame one which had
gone "must." It had been chained up as tame elephants always are
when their attack of "must" is due, but on the previous night it
had broken its chain and escaped. Its mahout, the only person who
could manage it when it was in that state, had set out in pursuit,
but he had taken the wrong direction and was now twelve hours'
journey away, and in the morning the elephant had suddenly
reappeared in the town. The Burmese population had no weapons
and were quite helpless against it. It had already destroyed somebody's bamboo hut, killed a cow and raided some fruit-stalls and
devoured the stock; also it had met the municipal rubbish van, and,
when the driver jumped out and took to his heels, had turned the
van over and inflicted violence upon it.

The Burmese sub-inspector and some Indian constables were
waiting for me in the quarter where the elephant had been seen.
It was a very poor quarter, a labyrinth of squalid bamboo huts,
thatched with palm-leaf, winding all over a steep hillside. I
remember that it was a cloudy stuffy morning at the beginning
of the rains. We began questioning the people as to where the
elephant had gone, and, as usual, failed to get any definite information. That is invariably the case in the East; a story always sounds
clear enough at a distance, but the nearer you get to the scene of
events the vaguer it becomes. Some of the people said that the
elephant had gone in one direction, some said that he had gone in
another, some professed not even to have heard of any elephant. I

---

in terrorem: Latin phrase meaning "in fear" or "to frighten"
must: a period of highly aggressive behavior triggered by mating instincts
mahout: an elephant keeper or trainer
labyrinth: a maze; a place full of complex, interconnected passageways
squalid: filthy

had almost made up my mind that the whole story was a pack of lies, when we heard yells a little distance away. There was a loud, scandalised cry of "Go away, child! Go away this instant!" and an old woman with a switch in her hand came round the corner of a hut, violently shooing away a crowd of naked children. Some more women followed, clicking their tongues and exclaiming; evidently there was something there that the children ought not to have seen. I rounded the hut and saw a man's dead body sprawling in the mud. He was an Indian, a black Dravidian coolie, almost naked, and he could not have been dead many minutes. The people said that the elephant had come suddenly upon him round the corner of the hut, caught him with its trunk, put its foot on his back and ground him into the earth. This was the rainy season and the ground was soft, and his face had scored a trench a foot deep and a couple of yards long. He was lying on his belly with arms crucified and head sharply twisted to one side. His face was coated with mud, the eyes wide open, the teeth bared and grinning with an expression of unendurable agony. (Never tell me, by the way, that the dead look peaceful. Most of the corpses I have seen looked devilish.) The friction of the great beast's foot had stripped the skin from his back as neatly as one skins a rabbit. As soon as I saw the dead man I sent an orderly to a friend's house nearby to borrow an elephant rifle. I had already sent back the pony, not wanting it to go mad with fright and throw me if it smelled the elephant.

The orderly came back in a few minutes with a rifle and five cartridges, and meanwhile some Burmans had arrived and told us that the elephant was in the paddy fields below, only a few hundred yards away. As I started forward practically the whole population of the quarter flocked out of their houses and followed me. They had seen the rifle and were all shouting excitedly that I was going to shoot the elephant. They had not shown much interest in the elephant when he was merely ravaging their homes, but it was different now that he was going to be shot. It was a bit of fun to them, as it would be to an English crowd; besides, they wanted the

---

Dravidian: a person from southern India
coolie: a laborer; the term is now considered to be offensive
paddy fields: rice fields

meat. It made me vaguely uneasy. I had no intention of shooting the elephant—I had merely sent for the rifle to defend myself if necessary—and it is always unnerving to have a crowd following you. I marched down the hill, looking and feeling a fool, with the rifle over my shoulder and an ever-growing army of people jostling at my heels. At the bottom, when you got away from the huts, there was a metalled road and beyond that a miry waste of paddy fields a thousand yards across, not yet ploughed but soggy from the first rains and dotted with coarse grass. The elephant was standing eighty yards from the road, his left side towards us. He took not the slightest notice of the crowd's approach. He was tearing up bunches of grass, beating them against his knees to clean them and stuffing them into his mouth.

I had halted on the road. As soon as I saw the elephant I knew with perfect certainty that I ought not to shoot him. It is a serious matter to shoot a working elephant—it is comparable to destroying a huge and costly piece of machinery—and obviously one ought not to do it if it can possibly be avoided. And at that distance, peacefully eating, the elephant looked no more dangerous than a cow. I thought then and I think now that his attack of "must" was already passing off; in which case he would merely wander harmlessly about until the mahout came back and caught him. Moreover, I did not in the least want to shoot him. I decided that I would watch him for a little while to make sure that he did not turn savage again, and then go home.

But at that moment I glanced round at the crowd that had followed me. It was an immense crowd, two thousand at the least and growing every minute. It blocked the road for a long distance on either side. I looked at the sea of yellow faces above the garish clothes—faces all happy and excited over this bit of fun, all certain that the elephant was going to be shot. They were watching me as they would watch a conjuror about to perform a trick. They did not

---

jostling: pushing and shoving
metalled: paved
miry: boggy; marshy
ploughed: variant spelling of *plowed*
garish: tastelessly bright; gaudy
conjuror: magician

like me, but with the magical rifle in my hands I was momentarily worth watching. And suddenly I realised that I should have to shoot the elephant after all. The people expected it of me and I had got to do it; I could feel their two thousand wills pressing me forward, irresistibly. And it was at this moment, as I stood there with the rifle in my hands, that I first grasped the hollowness, the futility of the white man's dominion in the East. Here was I, the white man with his gun, standing in front of the unarmed native crowd—seemingly the leading actor of the piece; but in reality I was only an absurd puppet pushed to and fro by the will of those yellow faces behind. I perceived in this moment that when the white man turns tyrant it is his own freedom that he destroys. He becomes a sort of hollow, posing dummy, the conventionalised figure of a sahib. For it is the condition of his rule that he shall spend his life in trying to impress the "natives" and so in every crisis he has got to do what the "natives" expect of him. He wears a mask, and his face grows to fit it. I had got to shoot the elephant. I had committed myself to doing it when I sent for the rifle. A sahib has got to act like a sahib; he has got to appear resolute, to know his own mind and do definite things. To come all that way, rifle in hand, with two thousand people marching at my heels, and then to trail feebly away, having done nothing—no, that was impossible. The crowd would laugh at me. And my whole life, every white man's life in the East, was one long struggle not to be laughed at.

But I did not want to shoot the elephant. I watched him beating his bunch of grass against his knees, with that preoccupied grand-motherly air that elephants have. It seemed to me that it would be murder to shoot him. At that age I was not squeamish about killing animals, but I had never shot an elephant and never wanted to. (Somehow it always seems worse to kill a *large* animal.) Besides, there was the beast's owner to be considered. Alive, the elephant was worth at least a hundred pounds; dead, he would only be worth the value of his tusks—five pounds, possibly. But I had got

futility: pointlessness
dominion: rule
sahib: a title meaning "master," which was once used to show respect to Europeans in India and other parts of Southeast Asia
resolute: firm; determined

to act quickly. I turned to some experienced-looking Burmans who had been there when we arrived, and asked them how the elephant had been behaving. They all said the same thing: he took no notice of you if you left him alone, but he might charge if you went too close to him.

It was perfectly clear to me what I ought to do. I ought to walk up to within, say, twenty-five yards of the elephant and test his behaviour. If he charged I could shoot, if he took no notice of me it would be safe to leave him until the mahout came back. But also I knew that I was going to do no such thing. I was a poor shot with a rifle and the ground was soft mud into which one would sink at every step. If the elephant charged and I missed him, I should have about as much chance as a toad under a steam-roller. But even then I was not thinking particularly of my own skin, only the watchful yellow faces behind. For at that moment, with the crowd watching me, I was not afraid in the ordinary sense, as I would have been if I had been alone. A white man mustn't be frightened in front of "natives"; and so, in general, he isn't frightened. The sole thought in my mind was that if anything went wrong those two thousand Burmans would see me pursued, caught, trampled on and reduced to a grinning corpse like that Indian up the hill. And if that happened it was quite probable that some of them would laugh. That would never do. There was only one alternative. I shoved the cartridges into the magazine and lay down on the road to get a better aim.

The crowd grew very still, and a deep, low, happy sigh, as of people who see the theatre curtain go up at last, breathed from innumerable throats. They were going to have their bit of fun after all. The rifle was a beautiful German thing with cross-hair sights. I did not then know that in shooting an elephant one should shoot to cut an imaginary bar running from ear-hole to ear-hole. I ought therefore, as the elephant was sideways on, to have aimed straight at his ear-hole; actually I aimed several inches in front of this, thinking the brain would be further forward.

When I pulled the trigger I did not hear the bang or feel the kick—one never does when a shot goes home—but I heard the devilish roar of glee that went up from the crowd. In that instant, in too short a time, one would have thought, even for the bullet to get there, a mysterious, terrible change had come over the elephant. He neither stirred nor fell, but every line of his body had altered. He looked suddenly stricken, shrunken, immensely old, as though the frightful impact of the bullet had paralysed him without knocking him down. At last, after what seemed a long time—it might have been five seconds, I dare say—he sagged flabbily to his knees. His mouth slobbered. An enormous senility seemed to have settled upon him. One could have imagined him thousands of years old. I fired again into the same spot. At the second shot he did not collapse but climbed with desperate slowness to his feet and stood weakly upright, with legs sagging and head drooping. I fired a third time. That was the shot that did for him. You could see the agony of it jolt his whole body and knock the last remnant of strength from his legs. But in falling he seemed for a moment to rise, for as his hind legs collapsed beneath him he seemed to tower upwards like a huge rock toppling, his trunk reaching skyward like a tree. He trumpeted, for the first and only time. And then down he came, his belly towards me, with a crash that seemed to shake the ground even where I lay.

I got up. The Burmans were already racing past me across the mud. It was obvious that the elephant would never rise again, but he was not dead. He was breathing very rhythmically with long rattling gasps, his great mound of a side painfully rising and falling. His mouth was wide open—I could see far down into caverns of pale pink throat. I waited a long time for him to die, but his breathing did not weaken. Finally I fired my two remaining shots into the spot where I thought his heart must be. The thick blood welled out of him like red velvet, but still he did not die. His body did not even jerk when the shots hit him, the tortured breathing continued without a pause. He was dying, very slowly and in great agony, but in some world remote from me where not even a bullet could damage him further. I felt that I had got to put an end to that dreadful noise. It seemed dreadful to see the great beast lying there, powerless to move and yet powerless to die, and not even to be able to finish him. I sent back for my small rifle and poured shot after shot into his heart and down his throat.

_____

senility: state of extreme infirmity due to old age

145

They seemed to make no impression. The tortured gasps continued as steadily as the ticking of a clock.

In the end I could not stand it any longer and went away. I heard later that it took him half an hour to die. Burmans were arriving with dahs and baskets even before I left, and I was told they had stripped his body almost to the bones by the afternoon.

Afterwards, of course, there were endless discussions about the shooting of the elephant. The owner was furious, but he was only an Indian and could do nothing. Besides, legally I had done the right thing, for a mad elephant has to be killed, like a mad dog, if its owner fails to control it. Among the Europeans opinion was divided. The older men said I was right, the younger men said it was a damn shame to shoot an elephant for killing a coolie, because an elephant was worth more than any damn Coringhee coolie. And afterwards I was very glad that the coolie had been killed; it put me legally in the right and it gave me a sufficient pretext for shooting the elephant. I often wondered whether any of the others grasped that I had done it solely to avoid looking a fool.

----

dahs: knives
Coringhee: a person from Coringa, India
pretext: a made-up reason; an excuse

No Witchcraft for Sale

Doris Lessing

A well-known campaigner against nuclear arms and against racial inequality in Africa, Doris Lessing was born to British parents in 1919 in what is now Iran. She was raised primarily in southern Rhodesia, now Zimbabwe, *in south-central Africa. In 2007 she was awarded the Nobel Prize in Literature. "No Witchcraft for Sale" was published in her 1964 collection,* African Stories.

The Farquars had been childless for years when little Teddy was born; and they were touched by the pleasure of their servants, who brought presents of fowls and eggs and flowers to the homestead when they came to rejoice over the baby, exclaiming with delight over his downy golden head and his blue eyes. They congratulated Mrs. Farquar as if she had achieved a very great thing, and she felt that she had—her smile for the lingering, admiring natives was warm and grateful.

Later, when Teddy had his first haircut, Gideon the cook picked up the soft gold tufts from the ground, and held them reverently in his hand. Then he smiled at the little boy and said: "Little Yellow Head." That became the native name for the child. Gideon and Teddy were great friends from the first. When Gideon had finished his work, he would lift Teddy on his shoulders to the shade of a big tree, and play with him there, forming curious little toys from twigs and leaves and grass, or shaping animals from wetted soil. When Teddy learned to walk it was often Gideon who crouched before him, clucking encouragement, finally catching him when he fell, tossing him up in the air till they both became breathless with laughter. Mrs. Farquar was fond of the old cook because of his love for her child.

---

downy: covered with soft hair
reverently: with great respect

There was no second baby; and one day Gideon said: "Ah, missus, missus, the Lord above sent this one; Little Yellow Head is the most good thing we have in our house." Because of that "we" Mrs. Farquar felt a warm impulse toward her cook; and at the end of the month she raised his wages. He had been with her now for several years; he was one of the few natives who had his wife and children in the compound and never wanted to go home to his kraal, which was some hundreds of miles away. Sometimes a small piccanin who had been born the same time as Teddy, could be seen peering from the edge of the bush, staring in awe at the little white boy with his miraculous fair hair and Northern blue eyes. The two little children would gaze at each other with a wide, interested gaze, and once Teddy put out his hand curiously to touch the black child's cheeks and hair.

Gideon, who was watching, shook his head wonderingly, and said: "Ah, missus, these are both children, and one will grow up to be a baas, and one will be a servant"; and Mrs. Farquar smiled and said sadly, "Yes, Gideon, I was thinking the same." She sighed. "It is God's will," said Gideon, who was a mission boy. The Farquars were very religious people; and this shared feeling about God bound servant and masters even closer together.

Teddy was about six years old when he was given a scooter, and discovered the intoxications of speed. All day he would fly around the homestead, in and out of flowerbeds, scattering squawking chickens and irritated dogs, finishing with a wide dizzying arc into the kitchen door. There he would cry: "Gideon, look at me!" And Gideon would laugh and say: "Very clever, Little Yellow Head." Gideon's youngest son, who was now a herdsboy, came especially up from the compound to see the scooter. He was afraid to come near it, but Teddy showed off in front of him. "Piccanin," shouted Teddy, "get out of my way!" And he raced in circles around the black child until he was frightened, and fled back to the bush.

---

kraal: a hut or a village of huts
piccanin: a derogatory term for a small black child
baas: "boss" or "master" in Afrikaans (a language used in South Africa, developed
     from seventeenth-century Dutch)
intoxications: thrills

"Why did you frighten him?" asked Gideon, gravely reproachful.

Teddy said defiantly: "He's only a black boy," and laughed. Then, when Gideon turned away from him without speaking, his face fell. Very soon he slipped into the house and found an orange and brought it to Gideon, saying: "This is for you." He could not bring himself to say he was sorry; but he could not bear to lose Gideon's affection either. Gideon took the orange unwillingly and sighed. "Soon you will be going away to school, Little Yellow Head," he said wonderingly, "and then you will be grown up." He shook his head gently and said, "And that is how our lives go." He seemed to be putting a distance between himself and Teddy, not because of resentment, but in the way a person accepts something inevitable. The baby had lain in his arms and smiled up into his face: The tiny boy had swung from his shoulders and played with him by the hour. Now Gideon would not let his flesh touch the flesh of the white child. He was kind, but there was a grave formality in his voice that made Teddy pout and sulk away. Also, it made him into a man: With Gideon he was polite, and carried himself formally, and if he came into the kitchen to ask for something, it was in the way a white man uses toward a servant, expecting to be obeyed.

But on the day that Teddy came staggering into the kitchen with his fists to his eyes, shrieking with pain, Gideon dropped the pot full of hot soup that he was holding, rushed to the child, and forced aside his fingers. "A snake!" he exclaimed. Teddy had been on his scooter, and had come to a rest with his foot on the side of a big tub of plants. A tree snake, hanging by its tail from the roof, had spat full into his eyes. Mrs. Farquar came running when she heard the commotion. "He'll go blind," she sobbed, holding Teddy close against her. "Gideon, he'll go blind!" Already the eyes, with perhaps half an hour's sight left in them, were swollen up to the size of fists: Teddy's small white face was distorted by great purple

---

reproachful: full of disapproval

oozing protuberances. Gideon said: "Wait a minute, missus, I'll get some medicine." He ran off into the bush.

Mrs. Farquar lifted the child into the house and bathed his eyes with permanganate. She had scarcely heard Gideon's words; but when she saw that her remedies had no effect at all, and remembered how she had seen natives with no sight in their eyes, because of the spitting of a snake, she began to look for the return of her cook, remembering what she heard of the efficacy of native herbs. She stood by the window, holding the terrified, sobbing little boy in her arms, and peered helplessly into the bush. It was not more than a few minutes before she saw Gideon come bounding back, and in his hand he held a plant.

"Do not be afraid, missus," said Gideon, "this will cure Little Yellow Head's eyes." He stripped the leaves from the plant, leaving a small white fleshy root. Without even washing it, he put the root in his mouth, chewed it vigorously, and then held the spittle there while he took the child forcibly from Mrs. Farquar. He gripped Teddy down between his knees, and pressed the balls of his thumbs into the swollen eyes, so that the child screamed and Mrs. Farquar cried out in protest: "Gideon, Gideon!" But Gideon took no notice. He knelt over the writhing child, pushing back the puffy lids till chinks of eyeball showed, and then he spat hard, again and again, into first one eye, and then the other. He finally lifted Teddy gently into his mother's arms, and said: "His eyes will get better." But Mrs. Farquar was weeping with terror, and she could hardly thank him: It was impossible to believe that Teddy could keep his sight. In a couple of hours the swellings were gone: The eyes were inflamed and tender but Teddy could see. Mr. and Mrs. Farquar went to Gideon in the kitchen and thanked him over and over again. They felt helpless because of their gratitude: It seemed they could do nothing to express it. They gave Gideon presents for his wife and children, and a big increase in wages, but these things

---

protuberances: bulges; bumps

bush: an area of wilderness; woods

permanganate: a type of salt that, when mixed with water, is used as a disinfectant or antiseptic

efficacy: effectiveness

writhing: twisting; squirming

could not pay for Teddy's now completely cured eyes. Mrs. Farquar said: "Gideon, God chose you as an instrument for His goodness," and Gideon said: "Yes, missus, God is very good."

Now, when such a thing happens on a farm, it cannot be long before everyone hears of it. Mr. and Mrs. Farquar told their neighbors and the story was discussed from one end of the district to the other. The bush is full of secrets. No one can live in Africa, or at least on the veld, without learning very soon that there is an ancient wisdom of leaf and soil and season—and, too, perhaps most important of all, of the darker tracts of the human mind—which is the black man's heritage. Up and down the district people were telling anecdotes, reminding each other of things that had happened to them.

"But I saw it myself, I tell you. It was a puff-adder bite. The kaffir's arm was swollen to the elbow, like a great shiny black bladder. He was groggy after a half a minute. He was dying. Then suddenly a kaffir walked out of the bush with his hands full of green stuff. He smeared something on the place, and next day my boy was back at work, and all you could see was two small punctures in the skin."

This was the kind of tale they told. And, as always, with a certain amount of exasperation, because while all of them knew that in the bush of Africa are waiting valuable drugs locked in bark, in simple-looking leaves, in roots, it was impossible to ever get the truth about them from the natives themselves.

The story eventually reached town; and perhaps it was at a sundowner party, or some such function, that a doctor, who happened to be there, challenged it. "Nonsense," he said. "These things get exaggerated in the telling. We are always checking up on this kind of story, and we draw a blank every time."

---

veld: grassy plain of southern Africa
anecdotes: personal stories
puff-adder: a species of poisonous snake
kaffir: a derogatory term for a black person in southern Africa
exasperation: frustration or annoyance
sundowner party: a cocktail party; an informal get-together at the end of a workday

Anyway, one morning there arrived a strange car at the homestead, and out stepped one of the workers from the laboratory in town, with cases full of test tubes and chemicals.

Mr. and Mrs. Farquar were flustered and pleased and flattered. They asked the scientist to lunch, and they told the story all over again, for the hundredth time. Little Teddy was there too, his blue eyes sparkling with health, to prove the truth of it. The scientist explained how humanity might benefit if this new drug could be offered for sale; and the Farquars were even more pleased: They were kind, simple people, who liked to think of something good coming about because of them. But when the scientist began talking of the money that might result, their manner showed discomfort. Their feelings over the miracle (that was how they thought of it) were so strong and deep and religious, that it was distasteful to them to think of money. The scientist, seeing their faces, went back to his first point, which was the advancement of humanity. He was perhaps a trifle perfunctory: It was not the first time he had come salting the tail of a fabulous bush secret.

Eventually, when the meal was over, the Farquars called Gideon into their living room and explained to him that this baas, here, was a Big Doctor from the Big City, and he had come all that way to see Gideon. At this Gideon seemed afraid; he did not understand; and Mrs. Farquar explained quickly that it was because of the wonderful thing he had done with Teddy's eyes that the Big Baas had come.

Gideon looked from Mrs. Farquar to Mr. Farquar, and then at the little boy, who was showing great importance because of the occasion. At last he said grudgingly: "The Big Baas want to know what medicine I used?" He spoke incredulously, as if he could not believe his old friends could so betray him. Mr. Farquar began explaining how a useful medicine could be made out of the root, and how it could be put on sale, and how thousands of people, black and white, up and down the continent of Africa, could be saved by the medicine when that spitting snake filled their eyes

---

trifle: a small bit
perfunctory: unthinking; automatic
salting the tail: an expression meaning "attempting to catch or capture"
incredulously: disbelievingly; in a shocked manner

with poison. Gideon listened, his eyes bent on the ground, the skin of his forehead puckering in discomfort. When Mr. Farquar had finished he did not reply. The scientist, who all this time had been leaning back in a big chair, sipping his coffee and smiling with skeptical good humor, chipped in and explained all over again, in different words, about the making of drugs and the progress of science. Also, he offered Gideon a present.

There was silence after this further explanation, and then Gideon remarked indifferently that he could not remember the root. His face was sullen and hostile, even when he looked at the Farquars, whom he usually treated like old friends. They were beginning to feel annoyed; and this feeling annulled the guilt that had been sprung into life by Gideon's accusing manner. They were beginning to feel that he was unreasonable. But it was at that moment that they all realized he would never give in. The magical drug would remain where it was, unknown and useless except for the tiny scattering of Africans who had the knowledge, natives who might be digging a ditch for the municipality in a ragged shirt and a pair of patched shorts, but who were still born to healing, hereditary healers, being the nephews or sons of the old witch doctors whose ugly masks and bits of bone and all the uncouth properties of magic were the outward signs of real power and wisdom.

The Farquars might tread on that plant fifty times a day as they passed from house to garden, from cow kraal to mealie field, but they would never know it.

But they went on persuading and arguing, with all the force of their exasperation; and Gideon continued to say that he could not remember, or that there was no such root, or that it was the wrong season of the year, or that it wasn't the root itself, but the spit from his mouth that had cured Teddy's eyes. He said all these things one after another, and seemed not to care they were contradictory. He was rude and stubborn. The Farquars could hardly recognize their

---

annulled: cancelled
municipality: a township or the government of a township
uncouth: uncivilized
cow kraal: an enclosed pen where cows are kept
mealie field: a place where corn is stored

153

gentle, lovable old servant in this ignorant, perversely obstinate African, standing there in front of them with lowered eyes, his hands twitching his cook's apron, repeating over and over whichever one of the stupid refusals that first entered his head.

And suddenly he appeared to give in. He lifted his head, gave a long, blank angry look at the circle of whites, who seemed to him like a circle of yelping dogs pressing around him, and said: "I will show you the root."

They walked single file away from the homestead down a kaffir path. It was a blazing December afternoon, with the sky full of hot rain clouds. Everything was hot: The sun was like a bronze tray whirling overhead, there was a heat shimmer over the fields, the soil was scorching underfoot, the dusty wind blew gritty and thick and warm in their faces. It was a terrible day, fit only for reclining on a veranda with iced drinks, which is where they would normally have been at that hour.

From time to time, remembering that on the day of the snake it had taken ten minutes to find the root, someone asked: "Is it much further, Gideon?" And Gideon would answer over his shoulder, with angry politeness: "I'm looking for the root, baas." And indeed, he would frequently bend sideways and trail his hand among the grasses with a gesture that was insulting in its perfunctoriness. He walked them through the bush along unknown paths for two hours, in that melting destroying heat, so that the sweat trickled coldly down them and their heads ached. They were all quite silent: the Farquars because they were angry, the scientist because he was being proved right again; there was no such plant. His was a tactful silence.

At last, six miles from the house, Gideon suddenly decided they had had enough; or perhaps his anger evaporated at that moment. He picked up, without an attempt at looking anything but casual, a handful of blue flowers from the grass, flowers that had been growing plentifully all down the paths they had come.

---

perversely obstinate: strangely stubborn
tactful: considerate; polite

He handed them to the scientist without looking at him, and marched off by himself on the way home, leaving them to follow him if they chose.

When they got back to the house, the scientist went to the kitchen to thank Gideon: He was being very polite, even though there was an amused look in his eyes. Gideon was not there. Throwing the flowers casually into the back of his car, the eminent visitor departed on his way back to his laboratory.

Gideon was back in his kitchen in time to prepare dinner, but he was sulking. He spoke to Mr. Farquar like an unwilling servant. It was days before they liked each other again.

The Farquars made inquiries about the root from their laborers. Sometimes they were answered with distrustful stares. Sometimes the natives said: "We do not know. We have never heard of the root." One, the cattle boy, who had been with them a long time, and had grown to trust them a little, said: "Ask your boy in the kitchen. Now, there's a doctor for you. He's the son of a famous medicine man who used to be in these parts, and there's nothing he cannot cure." Then he added politely: "Of course, he's not as good as the white man's doctor, we know that, but he's good for us."

After some time, when the soreness had gone from between the Farquars and Gideon, they began to joke: "When are you going to show us the snake root, Gideon?" And he would laugh and shake his head, saying, a little uncomfortably: "But I did show you, missus, have you forgotten?"

Much later, Teddy, as a schoolboy, would come into the kitchen and say: "You old rascal, Gideon! Do you remember that time you tricked us all by making us walk miles all over the veld for nothing? It was so far my father had to carry me!"

And Gideon would double up with polite laughter. After much laughing, he would suddenly straighten himself up, wipe his old eyes, and look sadly at Teddy, who was grinning mischievously at him across the kitchen: "Ah, Little Yellow Head, how you have grown! Soon you will be grown up with a farm of your own...."

---

eminent: distinguished; important

Marriage Is a Private Affair

Chinua Achebe

Chinua Achebe, of the Ibo (also called Igbo) people, was born in Nigeria in 1930. His writings often explore the struggles and tensions in postcolonial Nigerian society. He is best known for his 1958 novel Things Fall Apart. *"Marriage Is a Private Affair" was first published in 1952.*

"Have you written to your dad yet?" asked Nene one afternoon as she sat with Nnaemeka in her room at 16 Kasanga Street, Lagos.

"No. I've been thinking about it. I think it's better to tell him when I get home on leave!"

"But why? Your leave is such a long way off yet—six whole weeks. He should be let into our happiness now."

Nnaemeka was silent for a while, and then began very slowly as if he groped for his words: "I wish I were sure it would be happiness to him."

"Of course it must," replied Nene, a little surprised. "Why shouldn't it?"

"You have lived in Lagos all your life, and you know very little about people in remote parts of the country."

"That's what you always say. But I don't believe anybody will be so unlike other people that they will be unhappy when their sons are engaged to marry."

"Yes. They are most unhappy if the engagement is not arranged by them. In our case it's worse—you are not even an Ibo."

This was said so seriously and so bluntly that Nene could not find speech immediately. In the cosmopolitan atmosphere of the city it had always seemed to her something of a joke that a person's tribe could determine whom he married.

Lagos: the largest city in Nigeria, Africa
Ibo: people living mainly in southeastern Nigeria, who speak the Igbo language
cosmopolitan: sophisticated; composed of people from many parts of the world

At last she said, "You don't really mean that he will object to your marrying me simply on that account? I had always thought you Ibos were kindly disposed to other people."

"So we are. But when it comes to marriage, well, it's not quite so simple. And this," he added, "is not peculiar to the Ibos. If your father were alive and lived in the heart of Ibibio-land he would be exactly like my father."

"I don't know. But anyway, as your father is so fond of you, I'm sure he will forgive you soon enough. Come on then, be a good boy and send him a nice lovely letter…"

"It would not be wise to break the news to him by writing. A letter will bring it upon him with a shock. I'm quite sure about that."

"All right, honey, suit yourself. You know your father."

As Nnaemeka walked home that evening he turned over in his mind different ways of overcoming his father's opposition, especially now that he had gone and found a girl for him. He had thought of showing his letter to Nene but decided on second thoughts not to, at least for the moment. He read it again when he got home and couldn't help smiling to himself. He remembered Ugoye quite well, an Amazon of a girl who used to beat up all the boys, himself included, on the way to the stream, a complete dunce at school.

I have found a girl who will suit you admirably — Ugoye Nweke, the eldest daughter of our neighbor, Jacob Nweke. She has a proper Christian upbringing. When she stopped schooling some years ago her father (a man of sound judgment) sent her to live in the house of a pastor where she has received all the training a wife could need. Her Sunday school teacher has told me that she reads her Bible very fluently. I hope we shall begin negotiations when you come home in December.

Ibibio: a people of southeastern Nigeria, neighbors to the Ibo (Igbo) people
Amazon: in Greek mythology, a member of a tribe of legendary female warriors

On the second evening of his return from Lagos, Nnaemeka sat with his father under a cassia tree. This was the old man's retreat where he went to read his Bible when the parching December sun had set and a fresh, reviving wind blew on the leaves.

"Father," began Nnaemeka suddenly, "I have come to ask for forgiveness."

"Forgiveness? For what, my son?" he asked in amazement.

"It's about this marriage question."

"Which marriage question?"

"I can't—we must—I mean it is impossible for me to marry Nweke's daughter."

"Impossible? Why?" asked his father.

"I don't love her."

"Nobody said you did. Why should you?" he asked.

"Marriage today is different…"

"Look here, my son," interrupted his father, "nothing is different. What one looks for in a wife are a good character and a Christian background."

Nnaemeka saw there was no hope along the present line of argument.

"Moreover," he said, "I am engaged to marry another girl who has all of Ugoye's good qualities, and who…"

His father did not believe his ears. "What did you say?" he asked slowly and disconcertingly.

"She is a good Christian," his son went on, "and a teacher in a girls' school in Lagos."

"Teacher, did you say? If you consider that a qualification for a good wife I should like to point out to you, Emeka, that no Christian woman should teach. St. Paul in his letter to the Corinthians says that women should keep silence." He rose slowly from his seat and paced forward and backward. This was his pet subject, and he condemned vehemently those church leaders who encouraged women to teach in their schools. After he had spent his

---

cassia tree: a medium-sized leafy tree
parching: thirst-inducing; hot
disconcertingly: worryingly
vehemently: with great anger and passion

158

emotion on a long homily he at last came back to his son's engagement, in a seemingly milder tone.

"Whose daughter is she, anyway?"

"She is Nene Atang."

"What!" All the mildness was gone again. "Did you say Neneataga, what does that mean?"

"Nene Atang from Calabar. She is the only girl I can marry." This was a very rash reply and Nnaemeka expected the storm to burst. But it did not. His father merely walked away into his room. This was most unexpected and perplexed Nnaemeka. His father's silence was infinitely more menacing than a flood of threatening speech. That night the old man did not eat.

When he sent for Nnaemeka a day later he applied all possible ways of dissuasion. But the young man's heart was hardened, and his father eventually gave him up as lost.

"I owe it to you, my son, as a duty to show you what is right and what is wrong. Whoever put this idea into your head might as well have cut your throat. It is Satan's work." He waved his son away.

"You will change your mind, Father, when you know Nene."

"I shall never see her," was the reply. From that night the father scarcely spoke to his son. He did not, however, cease hoping that he would realize how serious was the danger he was heading for. Day and night he put him in his prayers.

Nnaemeka, for his own part, was very deeply affected by his father's grief. But he kept hoping that it would pass away. If it had occurred to him that never in the history of his people had a man married a woman who spoke a different tongue, he might have been less optimistic. "It has never been heard," was the verdict of an old man speaking a few weeks later. In that short sentence he spoke for all of his people. This man had come with others to commiserate with Okeke when news went round about his son's behavior. By that time the son had gone back to Lagos.

---

homily: sermon; lecture
Calabar: a city in southeastern Nigeria
perplexed: confused
commiserate: to sympathize; to share sadness with

"It has never been heard," said the old man again with a sad shake of his head.

"What did Our Lord say?" asked another gentleman. "Sons shall rise against their Fathers; it is there in the Holy Book."

"It is the beginning of the end," said another.

The discussion thus tending to become theological, Madubogwu, a highly practical man, brought it down once more to the ordinary level.

"Have you thought of consulting a native doctor about your son?" he asked Nnaemeka's father.

"He isn't sick," was the reply.

"What is he then? The boy's mind is diseased and only a good herbalist can bring him back to his right senses. The medicine he requires is *Amalile,* the same that women apply with success to recapture their husbands' straying affection."

"Madubogwu is right," said another gentleman. "This thing calls for medicine."

"I shall not call in a native doctor." Nnaemeka's father was known to be obstinately ahead of his more superstitious neighbors in these matters. "I will not be another Mrs. Ochuba. If my son wants to kill himself let him do it with his own hands. It is not for me to help him."

"But it was her fault," said Madubogwu. "She ought to have gone to an honest herbalist. She was a clever woman, nevertheless."

"She was a wicked murderess," said Jonathan, who rarely argued with his neighbors because, he often said, they were incapable of reasoning. "The medicine was prepared for her husband, it was his name they called in its preparation, and I am sure it would have been perfectly beneficial to him. It was wicked to put it into the herbalist's food, and say you were only trying it out."

Six months later, Nnaemeka was showing his young wife a short letter from his father:

———————————

theological: relating to matters of religion or faith
Amalile: a type of African plant
obstinately: stubbornly

160

*It amazes me that you could be so unfeeling as to send me your
wedding picture. I would have sent it back. But on further thought
I decided just to cut off your wife and send it back to you because I
have nothing to do with her. How I wish that I had nothing to do with
you either.*

When Nene read through this letter and looked at the mutilated
picture her eyes filled with tears, and she began to sob.

"Don't cry, my darling," said her husband. "He is essentially
good-natured and will one day look more kindly on our marriage."
But years passed and that one day did not come.

For eight years, Okeke would have nothing to do with his son,
Nnaemeka. Only three times (when Nnaemeka asked to come
home and spend his leave) did he write to him.

"I can't have you in my house," he replied on one occasion. "It
can be of no interest to me where or how you spend your leave—or
your life, for that matter."

The prejudice against Nnaemeka's marriage was not confined to
his little village. In Lagos, especially among his people who worked
there, it showed itself in a different way. Their women, when they
met at their village meeting, were not hostile to Nene. Rather, they
paid her such excessive deference as to make her feel she was not
one of them. But as time went on, Nene gradually broke through
some of this prejudice and even began to make friends among
them. Slowly and grudgingly they began to admit that she kept her
home much better than most of them.

The story eventually got to the little village in the heart of the
Ibo country that Nnaemeka and his young wife were a most happy
couple. But his father was one of the few people in the village who
knew nothing about this. He always displayed so much temper
whenever his son's name was mentioned that everyone avoided it
in his presence. By a tremendous effort of will he had succeeded
in pushing his son to the back of his mind. The strain had nearly
killed him but he had persevered, and won.

Then one day he received a letter from Nene, and in spite of
himself he began to glance through it perfunctorily until all of a

---

deference: respect

161

sudden the expression on his face changed and he began to read more carefully.

> ...*Our two sons, from the day they learnt that they have a grandfather, have insisted on being taken to him. I find it impossible to tell them that you will not see them. I implore you to allow Nnaemeka to bring them home for a short time during his leave next month. I shall remain here in Lagos*...

The old man at once felt the resolution he had built up over so many years falling in. He was telling himself that he must not give in. He tried to steel his heart against all emotional appeals. It was a reenactment of that other struggle. He leaned against a window and looked out. The sky was overcast with heavy black clouds and a high wind began to blow, filling the air with dust and dry leaves. It was one of those rare occasions when even Nature takes a hand in a human fight. Very soon it began to rain, the first rain in the year. It came down in large sharp drops and was accompanied by the lightning and thunder which mark a change of season. Okeke was trying hard not to think of his two grandsons. But he knew he was now fighting a losing battle. He tried to hum a favorite hymn but the pattering of large raindrops on the roof broke up the tune. His mind immediately returned to the children. How could he shut his door against them? By a curious mental process he imagined them standing, sad and forsaken, under the harsh angry weather— shut out from his house.

That night he hardly slept, from remorse—and a vague fear that he might die without making it up to them.

---

implore: beg
resolution: steadfastness; determination
forsaken: abandoned
remorse: feelings of guilt and regret

from NECTAR IN A SIEVE

Kamala Markandaya

Nectar in a Sieve, published in 1954, is the first novel by Indian author Kamala Markandaya. Written in first person, it tells the story of Rukmani, a woman from a small rural village in southern India, from the time when she is married until her husband's death many years later. It explores changes to traditional ways of life in the first half of the twentieth century in India. In this excerpt from the novel, Rukmani returns from the village where she and her husband Nathan have made a home. They have come to pay a visit to her dying mother. While in her parents' house, Rukmani encounters Kennington, a white doctor whose influence creates some of the many changes to Rukmani's life that the novel chronicles.

"Do not worry," they said. "You will be putting lines in your face." They still say it, but the lines are already there and they are silent about *that*. Kali said it, and I knew she was thinking of her own brood. Kunthi said it, and in her eyes lay the knowledge of her own children. Janaki said, morosely, she wished it could happen to her; a child each year was no fun. Only Nathan did not say it to me, for he was worried, too, and knew better. We did not talk about it, it was always with us: a chill fear that Ira was to be our only child.

My mother, whenever I paid her a visit, would make me accompany her to a temple, and together we would pray and pray before the deity, imploring for help until we were giddy. But the Gods have other things to do: they cannot attend to the pleas of every suppli-

---

morosely: gloomily
deity: idol; god
imploring: begging
giddy: dizzy
Gods: In the Hindu faith, various gods and goddesses represent aspects of the
    supreme deity

cant who dares to raise his cares to heaven. And so the years rolled by and we still had only one child, and that a daughter.

When Ira was nearing six, my mother was afflicted with consumption, and was soon so feeble that she could not rise from bed. Yet in the midst of her pain she could still think of me, and one day she beckoned me near and placed in my hand a small stone lingam, symbol of fertility.

"Wear it," she said. "You will yet bear many sons. I see them, and what the dying see will come to pass…be assured this is no illusion."

"Rest easy," I said. "You will recover."

She did not—no one expected she would—but she lingered for a long time. In her last months my father sent for the new doctor who had settled in the village. Nobody knew where he came from or who paid him, but there he was, and people spoke well of him, though he was a foreigner. As for my father, he would have called in the Devil himself to spare my mother any suffering. So it was in a house of sorrow that I first met Kennington, whom people called Kenny. He was tall and gaunt, with a pale skin and sunken eyes the colour of a king-fisher's wing, neither blue nor green. I had never seen a white man so close before, and so I looked my fill.

"When you have done with staring," he said coldly, "perhaps you will take me to your mother."

I started, for I had not realized I was goggling at him.

Startled, too, that he should have spoken in our tongue.

"I will show you," I said, stumbling in my confusion.

My mother knew no man could save her and she did not expect miracles. Between her and this man, young though he was, lay mutual understanding and respect, one for the other. He told her no lies, and she trusted him. He came often, sometimes even when he was not summoned; and his presence, as much as the powders

---

supplicant: one who prays or begs for help
afflicted: stricken; taken ill
consumption: tuberculosis, a potentially fatal disease of the lungs that makes
    breathing difficult
lingam: a symbolic trinket or charm
king-fisher: a small bird with brightly colored feathers
goggling: staring

and pills he made her take, gave my mother her ease. When she died it was in the same way, without a struggle, so that although we grieved for her our hearts were not torn by her suffering.

Before I left my village, I told him that for what he had done there could be no repayment. "Remember only," I said, "that my home is yours, and all in it."

He thanked me gravely, and as I turned to go he raised a hand to stop me.

"There is a look about you," he said. "It lies in your eyes and the mark is on your face. What is it?"

"Would you not grieve too," I said, "if the woman who gave you birth was no more than a handful of dust?"

"It is not that alone. The hurt is of longer standing. Why do you lie?"

I looked up and his eyes were on me. Surely, I thought, my mother has told him, for he knows; but as if he guessed my thoughts he shook his head. "No, I do not know. Tell me."

I held back. He was a foreigner, and although I no longer stood in awe of him, still the secret had been long locked up in my breast and would not come out easily.

"I have no sons," I said at last, heavily. "Only one child, a girl."

Once I had started the words flowed, I could not stop myself. "Why should it be?" I cried. "What have we done that we must be punished? Am I not clean and healthy? Have I not borne a girl so fair, people turn to gaze when she passes?"

"That does not seem to help you much," he said shortly. I waited. If he wishes to help me he can, I thought, so much faith had I in him. My heart was thumping out a prayer.

"Come and see me," he said at last. "It is possible I may be able to do something.... Remember, I do not promise."

My fears came crowding upon me again. I had never been to this kind of doctor; he suddenly became terrifying.

"You are an ignorant fool," he said roughly. "I will not harm you."

I slunk away, frightened of I know not what. I placed even more faith in the charm my mother had given me, wearing it constantly

---

slunk: moved without energy

165

between my breasts. Nothing happened. At last I went again to him, begging him to do what he could. He did not even remind me of the past.

Ira was seven when my first son was born, and she took a great interest in the newcomer. Poor child, it must have been lonely for her all those years. Kali's and Janaki's children were much older, and as for Kunthi, she preferred to keep aloof. Her son was a sturdy youngster and would have been a good playmate for my child; but, as the years went by, her visits to our house grew less and less frequent until at last we were meeting as strangers.

My husband was overjoyed at the arrival of a son; not less so, my father. He came, an old man, all those miles by cart from our village, to hold his grandson.

"Your mother would have been glad," he said. "She was always praying for you."

"She knew," I told him. "She said I would have many sons."

As for Nathan, nothing would do but that the whole village should know—as if they didn't already. On the tenth day from the birth he invited everybody to feast and rejoice with us in our good fortune. Kali and Janaki both came to help me prepare the food, and even Kunthi's reserve crumbled a little as she held up my son to show him to our visitors. Between us we prepared mounds of rice, tinting it with saffron and frying it in butter; made hot curries from chillies and dhal; mixed sweet, spicy dishes of jaggery and fruit; broiled fish; roasted nuts over the fire; filled ten gourds with coconut milk; and cut plantain leaves on which to serve the food. When all was ready we spread the leaves under the gaudy marriage pandal Nathan had borrowed for the occasion and ate and drank for long, merry hours. Afterwards Kunthi was persuaded to

---

reserve: calm or collected demeanor
tinting: coloring
dhal: a type of pea or lentil
jaggery: a type of raw sugar
gourds: large fruits that can be eaten or hollowed out to serve as containers for
    liquids
pandal: a structure built for use during the religious ceremonies of Hindus or
    Buddhists

166

play for us on her bulbul tara, which she did skillfully, plucking at the strings on her slender fingers and singing in a low, clear voice which people strained to hear, so that it was very quiet.

The baby, who had slept through all the clamour, woke up now in the sudden hush and began squalling. Kunthi stopped her thrumming. People crowded around me, trying to pat the baby who had caused all this excitement—although he was no beauty, with puckered face and mouth opened wide to emit shriek after shriek.

"Such a furore," Kali said. "One would think the child had wings, at the very least."

"Seven years we have waited," said Nathan, his eyes glinting, "wings or no wings."

The one person I had wanted most to see at our feast was not there. I had gone to seek him, but he was not to be found. "He goes and comes," they told me. "Nobody knows where or why." So I had to be content without him; but contentment cannot be forced, and Nathan noticed my preoccupation.

"What now?" he said. "Are you not happy? Would you have the moon too, as Kali would have wings?"

"Indeed no," I said, "it is just that I would have liked to see Kenny under our roof. He did so much for my mother." And for us, I thought, but could not say it; for at the beginning I had not wished my husband to know that I was putting myself in the hands of a foreigner, for I knew not what his reaction would be. I had consoled myself that it would be time enough to tell him if a child was born; and now I found I could not do it, because he would surely ask why I had not told him before.... What harm, I thought, if he does not know; I have not lied to him, there has just been this silence.

In our sort of family it is well to be the first-born: what resources there are, have later to be shared out in smaller and smaller portions. Ira had been fed well on milk and butter rice: Arjun too, for he was the first boy. But for those who came after, there was

---

bulbul tara: a stringed instrument sometimes called the Indian banjo
thrumming: strumming
preoccupation: distractedness

less and less. Four more sons I bore in as many years—Thambi, Murugan, Raja and Selvam. It was as if all the pent-up desires of my childless days were now bearing fruit. I was very fortunate, for they were, without exception, healthy; and in their infancy and childhood my daughter looked after them almost as much as I did. She was a great one for babies, handling them better than many a grown woman while she was still a child.

How quickly children grow! They are infants—you look away a minute and in that time they have left their babyhood behind. Our little girl ran about in the sun bare and beautiful as she grew, with no clothes to hamper her limbs or confine her movements. Then one day when she was five—long before Arjun was born—Nathan pointed her out to me as she played in the fields.

"Cover her," he said. "It is time."

I wanted to cry out that she was a baby still, but of course Nathan was right; she had left infancy forever. And so I made a skirt for her, weaving bright colours into the white cotton that she might like it, and so she did for a time, wearing it gladly, twirling it about her as she spun round and round; but when the novelty had worn off, she became fractious and wanted to tear it from her. It was nearly a month before she resigned herself to it.

With six children to feed we could no longer afford to eat all the vegetables we grew. Once a week I would cut and pack our garden produce, selecting the best and leaving the spoilt or bruised vegetables for ourselves, cover the basket with leaves and set off for the village. Old Granny was always glad to buy from me, and at first I would make straight for the corner of the street where she sat with gunny sack spread before her. The old lady would pick out the purple brinjals and yellow pumpkins, the shiny green and red chillies, feeling them with wrinkled fingers and complimenting me on their size.

"None like yours," she would say. "Such colour, such a bloom on them!" Perhaps she said it to everyone who came to her, but I would feel absurdly pleased and go away with my insides smiling.

---

hamper: hinder; get in the way of
fractious: cross; stubborn
gunny sack: a burlap bag
brinjals: eggplants

Then one day Biswas, the moneylender, stopped me in the street. I would have passed after a brief salutation, for among us there is a dislike of the moneylending class, but he stood squarely in the path.

"Ah, Rukmani," he said, "in a hurry as usual, I see."

"My children are not of age to be left alone for long," said I, speaking civilly.

"Yet surely you have time for a little business with me?"

"If you will tell me what business?"

"Buying and selling," he said, cackling, "Which is your business, as lending is mine."

"If you will make yourself clear," I said, "I will stay and hear; otherwise I must be on my way."

"Those vegetables," he said, "that Old Granny buys from you: What price does she pay you?"

"A fair price," I said, "and no haggling."

"I will pay you four annas a dozen for brinjals, and six annas each for pumpkins, if they are large." He was offering almost double what Old Granny paid.

I went away. The following week I sold almost my whole basket to him, keeping only a little for Old Granny. I did not like selling to him, although he paid me a better price. It was business and nothing else with him, never a word of chaff or a smile—or perhaps it was the flattery I missed—and I would much rather have had it the other way; but there you are, you cannot choose.

To my surprise Old Granny made no comment, beyond smiling reassuringly when I muttered guiltily that our needs at home were growing. In the beginning she may not have known, but when I sold her, week after week, one small pumpkin or half a dozen brinjals she must have guessed the truth. But she said nothing, nor did I for we both knew she could not afford to pay me more, and I could not afford to sell for less. As it was, we were going short of many

---

salutation: greeting
civilly: politely
cackling: laughing
haggling: bargaining; arguing over the price of something
annas: copper coins
chaff: friendly exchanges; chat or banter

things. We no longer had milk in the house, except for the youngest child; curds and butter were beyond our means except on rare occasions. But we never went hungry as some of the families were doing. We grew our own plantains and coconuts, the harvests were good and there was always food in the house—at least a bagful of rice, a little dhal, if no more. Then when the rice terraces were drained, there was the fish, spawned among the paddy, and what we could not eat, we dried and salted away. And every month I put away a rupee or two against the time Ira would be married. So we still could not grumble.

Change I had known before, and it had been gradual. My father had been a headman once, a person of consequence in our village: I had lived to see him relinquish this importance, but the alteration was so slow that we hardly knew when it came. I had seen both my parents sink into old age and death, and here too there was no violence. But the change that now came into my life, into all our lives, blasting its way into our village, seemed wrought in the twinkling of an eye.

Arjun came running to us with the news. He had run all the way from the village and we had to wait while he gulped in fresh air. "Hundreds of men," he gasped. "They are pulling down houses around the maidan and there is a long line of bullock carts carrying bricks."

The other children clustered round him, their eyes popping. Arjun swelled with importance. "I am going back," he announced. "There is a lot to be seen."

Nathan looked up from the grain he was measuring into the gunny bag for storing. "It is the new tannery they are building." he said. "I had heard rumours."

---

curds: coagulated milk, used to make cheese
plantains: fruits similar to bananas
terraces: shelves of land made level for the growing of crops
paddy: a flooded field where rice is grown
rupee: a unit of Indian currency
headman: leader of a tribe or group
maidan: an open field near a town
bullock carts: carts pulled by oxen
tannery: a workshop where animal hides are turned into leather goods

Arjun, torn between a desire to dash back and a craving to hear more from his father, teetered anxiously to and fro on his heels; but Nathan said no more. He put the grain away carefully in the granary, then he rose. "Come," he said. "We will see."

All the families were out: the news had spread quickly.

Kali and her husband, Kunthi and her boys, Janaki, surrounded by her numerous family, even Old Granny, had come out to see. Children were everywhere, dodging in and out of the crowd and crying out to each other in shrill excited voices. Startled pi-dogs added to the din. We formed a circle about the first arrivals, some fifty men or so, who were unloading bricks from the bullock carts. They spoke in our language, but with an intonation which made it difficult for us to understand them.

"Townspeople," Kali whispered to me. "They say they have travelled more than a hundred miles to get here." She was prone to exaggerate, and also believed whatever was told her.

In charge of the men was an overseer who looked and spoke like the men, but who was dressed in a shirt and trousers, and he had a hat on his head such as I had only seen Kenny wear before: a topee the colour of thatch. The others wore loincloths and turbans and a few wore shirts, but as the day wore on they doffed their shirts, one by one, until all were as our men.

The men worked well and quickly with many a sidelong glance at us; they seemed to enjoy having created such a stir and lured such a big audience. As for the overseer, he made much play of his authority, directing them with a loud voice and many gestures but doing not a stroke of work himself. Still, it must have been hot for him standing there waving his arms about, for the shirt he wore was sticking to his back now and then he would lift his hat as if to allow the wind to cool his scalp.

Until at last there was a commotion about the edges of the circle of which we were the inner ring. The crowd was parting, and as

---

pi-dogs: stray dogs
intonation: accent
topee: a lightweight hat
thatch: hay
doffed: removed
sidelong: sideways

the movement spread to us we gave way too, to let a tall white man through. He had on a white topee, and was accompanied by three or four men dressed like him in shorts. The overseer now came forward, bowing and scraping, and the red-faced one spoke to him rapidly but so low that we could not hear what he was saying. The overseer listened respectfully and then began telling us to go, not to disturb the men, although for so long he had been glad of many watchers. In our maidan, in our village he stood telling us to go.

"As if he owned us," muttered Kannan the chakkli. I think that already he foresaw his livelihood being wrested from him, for he salted and tanned his own skins, making them into chaplis for those in the village who wore them. So he stood his ground, glaring at the overseer and refusing to move, as did a few others who resented the haughty orders that poured from the man's lips; but most of us went, having our own concerns to mind.

Every day for two months the line of bullock carts came in laden with bricks and stones and cement, sheets of tin and corrugated iron, coils of rope and hemp. The kilns in the neighbouring villages were kept busy firing the bricks, but their output was insufficient, and the carts had to go farther afield, returning dusty and brick-filled. Day and night women twisted rope, since they could sell as much as they made, and traders waxed prosperous selling their goods to the workmen. They were very well paid, these men, some of them earning two rupees in a single day, whereas even in good times we seldom earned as much, and they bought lavishly: rice and vegetables and dhal, sweetmeats and fruit. Around the maidan they built their huts, for there was no other place for them, and into these brought their wives and children, making a community of their own. At night we saw their fires and by day we heard their noise, loud, ceaseless, clangour and din, chatter, sometimes a

---

chakkli: a leatherworker
chaplis: leather sandals
laden: filled
corrugated: grooved; ribbed
afield: away
clangour: loud noises

chanting to help them get a heavy beam into position, or hoist a load of tin sheeting to the roof.

Then one day the building was completed. The workers departed, taking with them their goods and chattels, leaving only the empty huts behind. There was a silence. In the unwonted quiet we all wondered apprehensively what would happen next. A week went by and another. Losing our awe we entered the building, poking into its holes and corners, looking into the great vats and drums that had been installed; then, curiosity slaked, we set about our old tasks on the land and in our homes.

There were some among the traders—those who had put up their prices and made their money—who regretted their going. Not I. They had invaded our village with clatter and din, had taken from us the maidan where our children played, and had made the bazaar prices too high for us. I was not sorry to see them go.

"They will be back," said Nathan, my husband, "or others will take their place. And did you not benefit from their stay, selling your pumpkins and plantains for better prices than you did before?"

"Yes," said I, for I had, "but what could I buy with the money with the prices so high everywhere? No sugar or dhal or ghee have we tasted since they came, and should have had none so long as they remained."

"Nevertheless," said Nathan, "they will be back; for you may be sure they did not take so much trouble only to leave a shell in our midst. Therefore it is well to accept these things."

"Never, never," I cried. "They may live in our midst but I can never accept them, for they lay their hands upon us and we are all turned from tilling to barter, and hoard our silver since we cannot spend it, and see our children go without the food that their children gorge, and it is only in the hope that one day things will be as

sheeting: pieces of cut metal
chattels: movable pieces of property
unwonted: unusual
slaked: satisfied
bazaar: market
ghee: clarified butter, commonly used in India for cooking
from tilling to barter: from farming to selling goods as merchants
gorge: feast on

173

they were that we have done these things. Now that they have gone let us forget them and return to our ways."

"Foolish woman," Nathan said. "There is no going back. Bend like the grass, that you do not break."

Our children had not seen us so serious, so vehement, before. Three of my sons huddled together in a corner staring at us with wide eyes; the two youngest lay asleep, one in Ira's arms, the other leaning heavily against her; and she herself sagged against the wall with their weight as she sat there on the floor. There was a look on her lovely soft face that pierced me.

"Ah well," I said, dissembling, "perhaps I exaggerate. If they return we shall have a fine dowry for our daughter, and that is indeed a good thing."

The lost look went from Ira's face. She was a child still, despite the ripeness of her thirteen years, and no doubt fancied a grand wedding even as I had done.

They came back. Not the same men who went, but others, and not all at once but slowly. The red-faced white man came back with a foreman, and took charge of everything. He did not live in the village but came and went, while his men took over the huts that had lain empty, the ones who came last settling beside the river, bringing their wives and children with them, or dotting the maidan even more thickly with the huts they built for themselves and their families

I went back to my home, thankful that a fair distance still lay between them and us, that although the smell of their brews and liquors hung permanently in the sickened air, still their noise came to us from afar.

"You are a queer being," Kunthi said, her brows flaring away from her eyes. "Are you not glad that our village is no longer a clump of huts but a small town? Soon there will be shops and

---

vehement: passionate
dissembling: lying
dowry: in many cultures, money paid by the bride's family to the family of the
    groom
fancied: imagined
queer: strange

tea stalls, and even a bioscope, such as I have been to before I was married. You will see."

"No doubt I will," I said. "It will not gladden me. Already my children hold their noses when they go by, and all is shouting and disturbance and crowds wherever you go. Even the birds have forgotten to sing, or else their calls are lost to us."

"You are a village girl," said Kunthi, and there were shadows of contempt moving behind her eyes. "You do not understand."

If I was a village girl, Kali and Janaki were too, and had no taste for the intruders; but after a while Janaki confessed that at least she now knew what to do with her sons, for the land could not take them all; and as for Kali, well, she had always been fond of an audience for her stories. So they were reconciled and threw the past away with both hands that they might be the readier to grasp the present, while I stood by in pain, envying such easy reconciliation and clutching in my own two hands the memory of the past, and accounting it a treasure.

I think the end of my daughter's carefree days began with the tannery. She had been used to come and go with her brothers, and they went whither they wished. Then one day, with many a meaningful wink, Kali told us that it was time we looked to our daughter.

"She is maturing fast," she said. "Do you not see the eyes of the young men lighting on her? If you are not careful you will not find it easy to get her a husband."

"My daughter is no wanton," Nathan replied. "Not only men but women look at her, for she is beautiful."

"She is that," Kali said handsomely. "Therefore look to her even more closely." There was no subduing Kali, as I well knew.

Thereafter, although we did not admit it to each other, we were more careful of Ira. Poor child, she was bewildered by the many injunctions we laid upon her, and the curtailing of her freedom tried her sorely, though not a word of complaint came from her.

---

bioscope: a movie theater
whither: wherever
wanton: careless or immoral person
injunctions: prohibitions; rules forbidding certain behavior

INDEX OF AUTHORS AND TITLES

ACKNOWLEDGMENTS

From BEOWULF, translated by Seamus Heaney. Copyright © 2000 by Seamus Heaney. Used by permission of W.W. Norton & Company, Inc.

"The Prologue," "The Pardoner's Tale," and "The Wife of Bath's Tale," 186 lines from THE CANTERBURY TALES by Geoffrey Chaucer, translated by Nevill Coghill (Penguin Classics 1951, Fourth revised edition 1977). Copyright 1951 by Nevill Coghill. Copyright © the Estate of Nevill Coghill, 1958, 1960, 1975, 1977.

"Darkness" and "When We Two Parted" from LORD BYRON, THE COMPLETED POETICAL WORKS, edited by Jerome J. McGann. Copyright 2000. Reprinted by permission of Oxford University Press.

"Do Not Go Gentle Into That Good Night" by Dylan Thomas, from THE POEMS OF DYLAN THOMAS. Copyright © 1952 by Dylan Thomas. Reprinted by permission of New Directions Publishing Corp.

"Eveline" from DUBLINERS by James Joyce. Copyright 1916 by B. W. Heubsch. Definitive text copyright © 1967 by the Estate of James Joyce. Used by permission of Viking Penguin, a division of Penguin Group (USA) Inc.

From THE ILIAD OF HOMER, translated by Richmond Lattimore. Copyright © 1951, The University of Chicago Press.

"An Irish Airman Foresees His Death." Reprinted with the permission of Scribner, a Division of Simon & Schuster, Inc, from THE COLLECTED WORKS OF W. B. YEATS, VOLUME 1: THE POEMS, REVISED, edited by Richard J. Finneran. Copyright © New York: Scribner 1997. All rights reserved.

"La Belle Dame sans Merci: A Ballad" and "Ode to Melancholy." Reprinted by permission of the publisher from JOHN KEATS COMPLETE POEMS, edited by Jack Stillinger, pp. 270–271, 283–284, Cambridge, Mass.: The Belknap Press of Harvard University Press. Copyright © 1978, 1982 by the President and Fellows of Harvard College.

"Lady in the Looking Glass: A Reflection" from A HAUNTED HOUSE AND OTHER SHORT STORIES by Virginia Woolf. Copyright 1944 and renewed 1972 by Harcourt, Inc. Reprinted by permission of Houghton Mifflin Harcourt Publishing Company.

"Marriage is a Private Affair" from GIRLS AT WAR AND OTHER STORIES by Chinua Achebe. Copyright © 1972, 1973 by Chinua Achebe. Used by permission of Doubelday, a division of Random House, Inc.

"Nectar in a Sieve" by Kamala Markandaya, Putnam, London, 1954. Reprinted with permission of the Estate of Kamala Markandaya.